KU-053-534

THE TATTER'S TREASURE CHEST

EDITED BY

Mary Carolyn Waldrep

DOVER PUBLICATIONS, INC., NEW YORK

Copyright © 1990 by Dover Publications, Inc.
All rights reserved under Pan American and International Copyright Conventions.

Published in Canada by General Publishing Company, Ltd., 30 Lesmill Road, Don Mills, Toronto, Ontario.

Published in the United Kingdom by Constable and Company, Ltd., 3 The Lanchesters, 162–164 Fulham Palace Road, London W6 9ER.

This Dover edition, first published in 1990, is a new selection of patterns from *Star Book of Crocheted, Knitted, Tatted, Book 15*, published by the American Thread Company, New York; *Star Book for the Home: Crocheted, Knitted, Tatted, Book 19*, published by the American Thread Company, 1942; *Tatted & Crocheted Designs, Star Book 30*, published by the American Thread Company, 1944; *Revised Beginner's Manual: Knitting, Crocheting, Tatting, Star Book 42*, published by the American Thread Company, 1946; *Treasure Chest of Crochet, Star Book No. 45*, published by the American Thread Company, 1946; *Gifts: Knitted and Crocheted, Star Gift Book No. 48*, published by the American Thread Company, 1946; *Doilies: Knitted, Crocheted, Tatted, Ruffled Doilies, Star Doily Book No. 151*, published by the American Thread Company, n.d.; *The Book of Tatting, Book 39*, published by The Spool Cotton Company, New York, 1934; *The Tatting Book, Book 111*, published by The Spool Cotton Company, 1938; *Tatting, Book No. 141*, published by The Spool Cotton Company, 1939; *New Things Happen to Tatting, Book No. 159*, published by The Spool Cotton Company, 1941; *Tatting: Luncheon Sets, Doilies, Collars, Edgings, Book No. 183*, published by The Spool Cotton Company, 1942; *Tatting: A Fascinating Book of Delicate Lace Designs, Book No. 207*, published by The Spool Cotton Company, 1944; *Tatting, Book No. 229*, published by The Spool Cotton Company, 1946; *Fine Crochet and Tatting, Book No. 259*, published by The Spool Cotton Company, 1949; *Learn to Tat, Book No. 330*, published by J. & P. Coats Ltd., Paisley, Scotland, n.d. A new Introduction has been written specially for this edition.

Manufactured in the United States of America
Dover Publications, Inc., 31 East 2nd Street, Mineola, N.Y. 11501

Library of Congress Cataloging-in-Publication Data

The Tatter's treasure chest / edited by Mary Carolyn Waldrep. — Dover ed.
    p.   cm. — (Dover needlework series)
  ISBN 0-486-26355-X
  1. Tatting—Patterns. I. Waldrep, Mary Carolyn. II. Series.
TT840.T38T37 1990
746.43'6041—dc20
                                            90-13823
                                                CIP

Table of Contents

Introduction

The history of tatting can be traced back over 200 years. It originally developed as an attempt to reproduce the expensive Venetian laces of the sixteenth century, but it has long since come to be appreciated for its own particular beauty.

Although fashions in needlework come and go, tatting has never gone completely out of vogue. Today, this delicate art is enjoying renewed popularity, and its enthusiasts are constantly in search of new designs. In this volume, we offer directions for over 100 tatted items of all kinds, taken from now hard-to-find instruction leaflets published by thread manufacturers in the first half of this century.

Despite its seeming intricacy, tatting is surprisingly easy to do. Only a few stitches need to be mastered in order to create beautiful tatted works of art. Complete instructions for tatting can be found on pages 94 and 95.

You may find that some of the threads listed in the instructions are no longer being made; however, many other threads that will give comparable results are readily available.

Once your tatted piece is complete, you should wash and block it. Use a mild soap and cool water. Squeeze the suds through the piece, but do not rub. Rinse two or three times in cool water. Using rustproof pins, pin the article right side down on a padded surface, pinning each picot, loop and scallop to shape. When the piece is nearly dry, press it through a damp cloth with a moderately hot iron. Do *not* allow the iron to rest on the stitches.

DOILIES

Starlight Doily

Measures 11 inches in diameter

Directions on page 24

SONATA

SPRINGTIME

Delectable Doilies

SONATA

. . . Materials: CLARK'S O.N.T. OR J. & P. COATS BEST SIX CORD MERCERIZED CROCHET, size 20, 1 ball of White or Ecru.

Completed doily measures about 4¼ x 5 inches.

CENTER . . . Use shuttle and ball of thread.

FIRST MOTIF . . . R of 4 ds, 3 p's sep. by 4 ds, 4 ds, cl. * Rw, ch of 8 ds, p, 8 ds. Rw, r of 4 ds, join to last p of previous r, 4 ds, p, 4 ds, p, 4 ds, cl. Repeat from * until 5th chain has been made. Make 6th r, joining as before, and also joining to 1st p of 1st r made. Rw. Make 6th ch as before, joining to base of 1st r made. Tie and cut.

Make second motif same as first, joining one ch to p on any ch of first motif. Make third motif same as last, joining one ch to p on ch of second motif, leaving 1 p free on second motif, between joining of 1st and 3rd motifs. Make fourth motif, joining 3 chains to corresponding p's on chains of first, second and third motifs, so that there are no free p's at center. This completes center of doily.

1st rnd of edge: * R of 4 ds, p, 4 ds, join to free p on ch of center, 4 ds, p, 4 ds, cl. Rw, ch of 10 ds, p, 10 ds. Rw. Repeat from * 13 times. Join last ch to base of 1st r. Tie and cut.

Outer edge: R of 4 ds, p, 4 ds, join to p on ch of previous rnd, 4 ds, p, 4 ds, cl. * Rw, ch of 4 ds, 3 p's sep. by 2 ds, 4 ds, rw. R of 4 ds, p, 4 ds, join to same p as previous r, 4 ds, p, 4 ds, cl. Rw, ch of 5 ds, 6 p's sep. by 2 ds, 5 ds. Rw, r of 4 ds, p, 4 ds, join to p of next ch, 4 ds, p, 4 ds, cl. Repeat from * around, joining last ch to base of 1st r made. Tie and cut.

SPRINGTIME

. . . Materials: CLARK'S O.N.T. OR J. & P. COATS BEST SIX CORD MERCERIZED CRO-CHET, size 20, 1 ball of White or Ecru.

Completed doily measures about 7 inches in diameter.

Use shuttle and ball of thread.

Center . . . R of 3 ds, 3 p's sep. by 3 ds, 3 ds, cl. Rw, ch of 9 ds, p, 9 ds. * Rw, r of 3 ds, join to last p of previous r,

Continued on next page

Springtime
Continued from page 8

3 ds, p, 3 ds, p, 3 ds, cl. Rw, ch of 9 ds, p, 9 ds. Repeat from * 8 more times, joining 3rd p of 10th r to 1st p of 1st r, and joining 10th ch to base of 1st r. Tie and cut. **1st rnd:** * R of 3 ds, p, 3 ds, join to p on ch of center, 3 ds, p, 3 ds, cl. Rw, ch of 5 ds, 3 p's sep. by 5 ds, 5 ds. Repeat from * 9 more times. Join last ch to base of 1st r. Tie and cut.

2nd rnd: R of 3 ds, p, 3 ds, join to 1st p on ch of 1st rnd, 3 ds, p, 3 ds, cl. * Rw, ch of 8 ds. R of 6 ds, p, 6 ds, cl. Ch of 6 ds. Rw, r of 3 ds, join to p of adjacent r, 3 ds, join to 2nd p on ch of 1st rnd, 3 ds, p, 3 ds, cl. Rw, ch of 6 ds. R of 6 ds, p, 6 ds. Ch of 6 ds. Rw, r of 3 ds, join to p of adjacent r, 3 ds, join to 3rd p on ch of 1st rnd. 3 ds, p. 3 ds, cl. Rw, ch of 6 ds. R of 6 ds, p, 6 ds, cl. Ch of 6 ds. Rw, r of 3 ds, join to p of adjacent r, 3 ds, join to 1st p of next ch of 1st rnd, 3 ds, p, 3 ds, cl. Repeat from * around, joining 3rd p of 30th r to 1st p of 1st r, and joining last ch to base of 1st r. Tie and cut.

3rd rnd: R of 6 ds, join to free p of r on 2nd rnd, 6 ds, cl. R of 6 ds, join to free p of next r of 2nd rnd, 6 ds, cl. * Rw, ch of 8 ds. R of 6 ds, p, 6 ds, cl. Ch of 8 ds. Rw, r of 6 ds, join to same p as previous r, 6 ds, cl. R of 6 ds, join to p of next r of 2nd rnd, 6 ds, cl. Repeat from * around, joining last ch to base of 1st r. Tie and cut. **4th rnd:** R of 4 ds, 3 p's sep. by 4 ds, 4 ds, cl. * R of 4 ds, join to last p of adjacent r, 2 ds, 5 p's sep. by 2 ds, 4 ds, cl. R of 4 ds, join to last p of previous r, 4 ds, 2 p's sep. by 4 ds, 4 ds, cl. Rw, ch of 5 ds, p, 5 ds, join to free p of r on 3rd rnd, 5 ds, p, 5 ds. Rw, r of 4 ds, p. 4 ds, join to center p of adjacent r, 4 ds, p, 4 ds, cl. Repeat from * around, joining last ch to base of 1st r. Tie and cut.

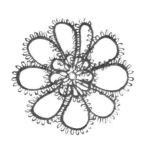

Cluster Doily

. . . **Materials:** CLARK'S O.N.T. OR J. & P. COATS BEST SIX CORD MERCERIZED CROCHET, size 20, 1 ball of White or Ecru.

A piece of linen, 8 inches square.

Completed doily measures about 9½ inches in diameter. Edging measures about 1 inch wide.

Cut circle of linen 7½ inches in diameter, and hem. Use shuttle and ball of thread. **1st rnd:** R of 4 ds, 3 p's sep. by 4 ds, 4 ds, cl (1st ring). * Rw, sp (⅛-inch). R of 4 ds, p, 4 ds, cl. Rw, sp, r of 4 ds, join to last p of adjacent r, 4 ds, p, 4 ds, p, 4 ds, cl (2nd ring). Rw, sp, r of 4 ds, join to p of adjacent r, 2 ds, 5 p's sep. by 2 ds, 4 ds, cl. Rw, sp, r of 4 ds, join to last p of adjacent r, 4 ds, p, 4 ds, p, 4 ds, cl (3rd ring). Rw, sp, r of 4 ds, join to last p of adjacent r, 4 ds, cl. Rw, sp, r of 4 ds, join to last p of adjacent r, 4 ds, p, 4 ds, p, 4 ds, cl.

Repeat from * until piece measures 26 inches, making edging into a circle by joining 3rd ring to the 1st p on 1st ring made, rw, sp, r of 4 ds, join to last p of adjacent r, 4 ds, cl. Tie and cut. **2nd rnd:** * R of 4 ds, 3 p's sep. by 4 ds, 4 ds, cl. Rw, make a ch of 5 ds, join to center p of 3rd ring of 1st rnd, 5 ds, join to center p of 2nd ring of 1st rnd. 5 ds, join to center p of 1st ring of 1st rnd, 5 ds. Let ball hang. Rw and repeat from * around. Join to 1st r of 2nd rnd. Tie and cut. Sew to linen.

Limelight

MATERIALS:

CLARK'S O.N.T. or J. & P. COATS BEST SIX CORD MERCERIZED CROCHET, size 20, 1 ball of White or Ecru.

Completed doily measures about 9½ inches long, by 7 inches wide.

First Motif . . . R of 2 ds, 5 p's sep. by 2 ds, 4 ds, lp (¼ inch high), 4 ds, 5 p's sep. by 2 ds, 2 ds, cl. R of 10 ds, 3 p's sep. by 5 ds, 10 ds, cl. * Rw, leave no sp, r of 10 ds, 3 p's sep. by 5 ds, 10 ds, cl, join to base of last r. Sp (⅜ inch), r of 4 ds, join to p of adjacent r, 8 ds, p, 4 ds, p, 8 ds, cl. Rw, leave no sp, r of 4 ds, join to p of adjacent r, 8 ds, p, 4 ds, p, 8 ds, cl, join to base of last r. Sp (¼ inch), r of 3 ds, join to p of adjacent r, 7 ds, p, 3 ds, p, 7 ds, cl. Rw, leave no sp, r of 3 ds, join to p of adjacent r, 7 ds, p, 3 ds, p, 7 ds, cl, join to base of last r. Sp (⅛ inch), r of 3 ds, join to p of adjacent r, 7 ds, p, 7 ds, join to corresponding p of next r, 3 ds, cl. Tie and cut (spray made). R of 2 ds, 4 p's sep. by 2 ds, 2 ds, join to corresponding p of 1st r of previous spray, 4 ds, join to lp, 4 ds, 5 p's sep. by 2 ds, 2 ds, cl. Rw, r of 10 ds, join to corresponding p of next r of previous spray, 5 ds, join to next p, 5 ds, p, 10 ds, cl. Repeat from * until there are 6 sprays in all, joining last spray to p's of both 5th and 1st sprays.

Second Motif . . . Same as First Motif until 7 r's of 1st spray have been made. Sp (⅛ inch), r of 3 ds, join to p of adjacent r, 7 ds, join to free p at end of any spray of First Motif, 7 ds, join to corresponding p of next r of Second Motif, 3 ds, cl. Tie and cut. Work 2nd spray same as 2nd spray of First Motif, but joining last r to next spray of First Motif same as previous spray was joined. Complete Second Motif same as First Motif (no more joinings).

Third Motif . . . Same as Second Motif joining 1st spray to spray of First Motif preceding 1st joining of First and Second Motifs, join 2nd spray to same p where 1st spray of Second Motif was joined, join 3rd spray to next spray of Second Motif.

Fourth Motif . . . Same as Second Motif, joining to Second and Third Motifs the same way that Third Motif was joined to First and Second Motifs.

Fill-in-Motif . . . R of 4 ds, 9 p's sep. by 2 ds, 4 ds, cl. R of 4 ds, join to adjacent p of previous r, 2 ds, p, 2 ds, p, 2 ds, join to 1st free p of any spray (counting from center of motif), 2 ds, 5 p's sep. by 2 ds, 4 ds, cl. R of 4 ds, join to adjacent p of previous r, 2 ds, 4 p's sep. by 2 ds, 2 ds, join to 1st free p (from center) of spray of next motif, 2 ds, 3 p's sep. by 2 ds, 4 ds, cl. R of 4 ds, join to adjacent p of previous r, 2 ds, 8 p's sep. by 2 ds, 4 ds, cl. R of 4 ds, join to adjacent p of previous r, 2 ds, p, 2 ds, p, 2 ds, join to next spray as before, 2 ds, 5 p's sep. by 2 ds, 4 ds, cl. R of 4 ds, join to adjacent p of previous r, 2 ds, 4 p's sep. by 2 ds, 2 ds, join to next spray, 2 ds, p, 2 ds, p, 2 ds, join to adjacent p of 1st r, 4 ds, cl. Tie and cut. Fill in all sps between motifs in same way.

Sunburst

MATERIALS:

CLARK'S O.N.T. or J. & P. COATS BEST SIX CORD MERCERIZED CROCHET, size 30, 1 ball of White or Ecru, or 2 balls of any color.

Completed doily measures about 8 inches in diameter.

Use shuttle and ball of thread.

1st rnd: Sr of 4 ds, lp (½ inch high), 4 ds, cl. Ch of 10 ds. Rw, lr of 6 ds, p, 5 ds, p, 5 ds, p, 6 ds, cl. Ch of 10 ds. * Rw, sr of 4 ds, join to lp, 4 ds, cl. Ch of 10 ds. Rw, lr of 6 ds, join to adjacent p of previous lr, 5 ds, p, 5 ds, p, 6 ds, cl. Ch of 10 ds. Repeat from * until there are 16 sr's and 16 lr's, joining last lr to 1st p of 1st lr. Join last ch to base of 1st sr. Tie and cut. **2nd rnd:** Lr of 6 ds,

p (slightly longer than in previous row), 5 ds, join to any free p of 1st rnd, 5 ds, p, 6 ds, cl. * Rw, ch of 8 ds, p, 8 ds. Rw, lr of 6 ds, join to adjacent p of previous lr, 5 ds, join to next free p of 1st rnd, 5 ds, p, 6 ds, cl. Repeat from * around joining last ch to base of 1st lr. Tie and cut.

First Point . . . R of 3 ds, 3 p's sep. by 3 ds, 3 ds, cl. R of 3 ds, join to adjacent p of previous r, 3 ds, join to free p of 2nd rnd, 3 ds, p, 3 ds, cl. R of 3 ds, join to adjacent p of previous r, 3 ds, p, 3 ds, p, 3 ds, cl. Rw, ch of 4 ds, p, 4 ds. Rw, r of 4 ds, join to adjacent p of previous r, 4 ds, p, 4 ds, p, 4 ds, cl. Rw, ch of 5 ds, p, 5 ds. Rw, r of 5 ds, join to adjacent p of previous r, 5 ds, p, 5 ds, p, 5 ds, cl. Rw, ch of 6 ds, p, 6 ds. Rw, r of 6 ds, join to adjacent p of previous r, 6 ds, p, 6 ds, p, 6 ds, cl. Rw, ch of 6 ds,

p, 6 ds. Rw, r of 5 ds, join to adjacent p of previous r, 5 ds, p, 5 ds, p, 5 ds, cl. Rw, ch of 5 ds, p, 5 ds. Rw, r of 4 ds, join to adjacent p of previous r, 4 ds, p, 4 ds, p, 4 ds, cl. Rw, ch of 4 ds, p, 4 ds. Rw, r of 3 ds, join to adjacent p of previous r, 3 ds, p, 3 ds, p, 3 ds, cl. * R of 3 ds, join to adjacent p of previous r, 3 ds, p, 3 ds, p, 3 ds, cl. Repeat from * once more. Rw, ch of 4 ds, join to p of adjacent ch, 4 ds. Rw, r of 4 ds, join to adjacent p of previous r, 4 ds, p, 4 ds, p, 4 ds, cl. Rw, ch of 5 ds, join to p of adjacent ch, 5 ds. Rw, r of 5 ds, join to adjacent p of previous r, 5 ds, p, 5 ds, p, 5 ds, cl. Rw, ch of 6 ds, join to p of adjacent ch, 6 ds. Rw, r of 6 ds, join to adjacent p of previous r, 6 ds, p, 6 ds, p, 6 ds, cl. Rw, ch of 6 ds, join to p of adjacent ch, 6 ds. Rw, r of 5 ds, join to adjacent p of previous r, 5 ds, p, 5 ds,

Continued on page 24

Duet Doily

COATS CHAIN ⊙ MERCER-CROCHET NO. 20 (20 Gr). 1 BALL SELECTED COLOUR. 1 BALL EACH OF TWO CONTRASTING COLOURS. TATTING SHUTTLE.

MEASUREMENT: 11 in. in diameter.

With selected colour, tie ball and shuttle threads together.

1st Row: R of 4 ds, 3 p's sep by 4 ds, 4 ds, cl. Rw, * ch of 3 ds, 4 p's sep by 2 ds, 3 ds, rw, r of 4 ds, join to last p of previous r, 4 ds, 2 p's sep by 4 ds, 4 ds, cl, rw ; repeat from * 8 times more, joining last p of last r to first p of first r, ch of 3 ds, 4 p's sep by 2 ds, 3 ds, join to base of first r. Tie and cut.

2nd Row: Tie ball and shuttle threads together. R of 8 ds, join to first p of first ch of first row, 8 ds, cl, * rw, ch of 7 ds, r of 8 ds, p, 8 ds, cl, ch of 7 ds, rw, r of 8 ds, miss one p, join to next p of same ch, 8 ds, cl, rw, ch of 7 ds, r of 8 ds, p, 8 ds, cl. Ch of 7 ds, rw, r of 8 ds, join to first p of next ch of first row, 8 ds, cl ; repeat from * ending with rw, ch of 7 ds, r of 8 ds, p, 8 ds, cl, ch of 7 ds, join to base of first r. Tie and cut.

3rd Row: With selected colour in shuttle and one of the contrasting balls tie threads together. * R of 4 ds, p, 4 ds, join to p of r of second row, 4 ds, p, 4 ds, cl. Rw, ch of 4 ds, 3 p's sep by 4 ds, 4 ds, rw ; repeat from * joining last ch to base of first r. Tie and cut.

4th Row: With selected colour in both shuttle and ball tie threads together. * R of 8 ds, join to p of ch of previous row, 8 ds, cl, rw, ch of 4 ds, p, 4 ds, rw ; repeat from * joining last ch to base of first r. Tie and cut.

5th Row: With selected colour in shuttle. * R of 8 ds, join to p of ch of previous row, 8 ds, cl, rw, sp of ½ in., r of 8 ds, p, 8 ds, cl, rw, sp of ½ in. ; repeat from *, join to base of first r. Tie and cut.

6th Row: With selected colour in shuttle and other contrasting colour on ball tie threads together. * R of 4 ds, p, 4 ds, join to p of r of previous row, 4 ds, p, 4 ds, cl, rw, ch of 3 ds, 3 p's sep by 3 ds, 3 ds, rw ; repeat from * joining last ch to base of first r. Tie and cut.

7th Row: With selected colour in shuttle and ball tie threads together. * R of 4 ds, p, 4 ds, join to centre p of ch of previous row, 4 ds, p, 4 ds, cl, rw, ch of 3 ds, 3 p's sep by 3 ds, 3 ds, rw ; repeat from * joining last ch to base of first r. Tie and cut.

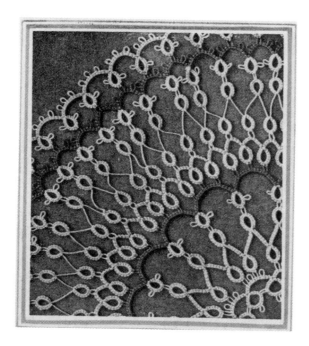

Spiderweb Dresser Set

This looks more complicated than it really is. After working the first three rows of rings and chains it is only a matter of making rings with spaces between, which get longer as the doily grows.

COATS CHAIN ⚙ MERCER CROCHET NO. 40 (20 Gr). 1 BALL SELECTED COLOUR, TATTING SHUTTLE.

MEASUREMENTS
Round Doily—11 ins. in diameter.
Oval Doily—10 ins. × 16 ins.

ROUND DOILY (Make 2).

STAR
Tie ball and shuttle threads together, r of 8 ds, 1 p, 8 ds, cl. * Rw, ch of 4 ds, p, 6 ds, p, 4 ds. Rw, r of 8 ds, join to l p of first r, 8 ds, cl ; repeat from * 3 times more. Rw, ch of 4 ds, p, 6 ds, p, 4 ds. Join to base of first r. Tie and cut.

1st Row : R of 8 ds, join to any p of star, 8 ds, cl. * Rw, ch of 4ds, 1 p, 6 ds, 1 p, 4 ds. Rw, r of 8 ds, join to next p on star, 8 ds, cl ; repeat from * joining last ch to base of first r. Tie and cut.

2nd Row : As first row, joining to l p of first row.

3rd Row : R of 4 ds, join to any p on previous row, 4 ds, cl. * Sp of ¾ in., r of 4 ds, join to next p on previous row, 4 ds, cl ; repeat from * to end of row. Hereafter mark the end of each row.

4th Row : * Sp of ¾ in., r of 4 ds, join to thread between next 2 r's on previous row, 4 ds, cl ; repeat from * to end of row.

5th to 9th Row : Work same as 4th row, only making the sp between r's ¼ in. longer.

10th Row : * Sp of ¾ in., r of 4 ds, p, 4 ds, cl, sp of ¾ in., r of 4 ds, join to sp between next 2 r's on previous row, 4 ds, cl ; repeat from * ending with sp of ¾ in., r of 4 ds, p, 4 ds, cl, sp of ¾ in., join to r of previous row. Tie and cut.

OVAL DOILY

1st Row : R of 8 ds, 1 p, 8 ds, cl. * Rw, ch of (4 ds, p) twice, 4 ds. Rw, r of 8 ds, join to 1 p of

Continued on page 15

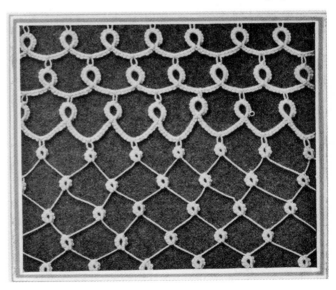

Tatted Picot

Materials Required:
AMERICAN THREAD COMPANY
"GEM" MERCERIZED CROCHET COTTON,
  Article 35, Size 50
1 ball White or
"STAR" TATTING CROCHET, Article 125
2 Balls White or color of your choice
Tatting Shuttle
App. size: 10¾ inches in diameter for "GEM" Size 50; 9 inches in diameter for "STAR" TATTING CROCHET

R, 3 ds, 3 p sep by 3 ds, 3 ds, cl r, turn, ¼ inch space. R, 3 ds, 3 p sep by 3ds, 3 ds, cl r. R, 4 ds, join to last p of last r, 3 ds, 2 p sep by 3 ds, 4 ds, cl r. R, 3 ds, join to last p of last r, 3 ds, 2 p sep by 3 ds, cl r (clover), turn, ¼ inch space. * R, 3 ds, join to last p of last single r, 3 ds, 2 p sep by 3 ds, 3 ds, cl r, turn, ¼ inch space. Work a clover joining center p of 1st r to center p of 3rd ring of last clover, turn, ¼ inch space. Repeat from * until there are 7 single rings at center and 7 clovers, turn, ¼ inch space. R, 3 ds, join to last p of single r, 3 ds, p, 3 ds, join to 1st p of 1st r, 3 ds, cl r, turn, ¼ inch space. Work 1st 2 rings of clover. R, 3 ds, join to last p of last r, 3 ds, join to corresponding p of 1st clover, 3 ds, p, 3 ds, cl r, tie and cut. 2nd ROUND: R, 4 ds, join to any free p, 4 ds, cl r, turn, ¼ inch space. R, 4 ds, p, 4 ds, cl r, ¼ inch space. R, 7 ds, p, 7 ds, cl r, ¼ inch space. * R, 12 ds, p, 12 ds, cl r. Repeat from * twice, ** turn, ¼ inch space. R, 7 ds, p, 7 ds, cl r, ¼ inch space. R, 4 ds, p, 4 ds, cl r, ¼ inch space. R, 4 ds, join to next free p of 1st round, 4 ds, cl r, turn, ¼ inch space. R, 4 ds, join to corresponding p of next to last r, 4 ds, cl r, ¼ inch space. R, 7 ds, join to corresponding p of corresponding r, 7 ds, cl r, ¼

inch space. R, 12 ds, join to 1st p of last large r, 12 ds, cl r. * R, 12 ds, p, 12 ds, cl r. Repeat from * once, turn, ¼ inch space. R, 7 ds, p, 7 ds, cl r, ¼ inch space. R, 4 ds, p, 4 ds, cl r, ¼ inch space. R, 4 ds, join to same p of same r of 1st round, 4 ds, cl r, turn, ¼ inch space. R, 4 ds, join to corresponding p of corresponding r, 4 ds, cl r, ¼ inch space. R, 7 ds, join to corresponding p of corresponding r, 7 ds, cl r, ¼ inch space. R, 12 ds, join to p of last large r, 12 ds, cl r. * R, 12 ds, p, 12 ds, cl r. Repeat from * once. Repeat from ** all around ending to correspond, tie and cut. 3rd ROUND: R, 5 ds, p, 8 ds, join to any free p of 2nd round, 8 ds, p, 5 ds, cl r, turn, ¼ inch space. R, 5 ds, p, 8 ds, p, 8 ds, p, 5 ds, cl r, turn, ¼ inch space. R, 5 ds, join to last p of 1st r, 8 ds, p, 8 ds, p, 5 ds, cl r, turn, ¼ inch space. R, 5 ds, join to last p of 2nd r, 8 ds, p, 8 ds, p, 5 ds, cl r, turn, ¼ inch space. R, 5 ds, join to last p of 3rd r, 8 ds, p, 8 ds, p, 5 ds, cl r, turn, ¼ inch space. R, 5 ds, join to last p of 4th r, 8 ds, p, 8 ds, p, 5 ds, cl r, turn, ¼ inch space. R, 5 ds, join to last p of 5th r, 8 ds, join to next free p of 2nd round, 8 ds, p, 5 ds, cl r, turn, ¼ inch space. Continue all around in same manner ending round to correspond, join, tie and cut. 4th ROUND: R, 3 ds, join to any free p of 3rd round, 3 ds, cl r, * turn, ¼ inch space. R, 3 ds, p, 3 ds, cl r, turn, ¼ inch space. R, 3 ds, join to next free p of 3rd round, 3 ds, cl r. Repeat from * all around ending to correspond, tie and cut. 5th ROUND: R, 10 ds, join to any p of 4th round, 10 ds, cl r, ** turn, ¼ inch space. R, 10 ds, p, 10 ds, cl r, turn, ¼ inch space. * R, 3 ds, join to next p of 4th round, 3 ds, cl r, turn, ¼ inch space. R, 3 ds, p, 3 ds, cl r, turn, ¼ inch space. Repeat from * 3 times. R, 3 ds, join to next p of 4th round, 3 ds, cl r, turn, ¼ inch space. R, 10 ds, p, 10 ds, cl r, turn, ¼ inch space. R, 10 ds, join to next p of 4th round, 10 ds, cl r. Repeat from ** all around, tie and cut. 6th ROUND: R, 10 ds, join to p of large r, 10 ds, cl r, ** turn, ¼ inch space. R, 10 ds, p, 10 ds, cl r, turn, ¼ inch space. R, 3 ds, join to p of small r, 3 ds, cl r, * turn, ¼ inch space. R, 3 ds, p, 3 ds, cl r, turn, ¼ inch space. R, 3 ds, join to p of next small r, 3 ds, cl r. Repeat from * twice, turn, ¼ inch space. R, 10 ds, p, 10 ds, cl r, turn, ¼ inch space. R, 10 ds, join to p of large r, 10 ds, cl r, turn, * ¼ inch space. R, 3 ds, p, 3 ds, cl r. Repeat from * 3 times, turn, ¼ inch space. R, 10 ds, join to p of next large r, 10 ds, cl r. Repeat from ** all around ending to correspond, tie and cut. 7th ROUND: R, 10 ds, join to p of large r of 6th round, 10 ds, cl r, turn, ¼ inch space. R, 10 ds, p, 10 ds, cl r, turn, * ¼ inch space. R, 3 ds, join to p of next small r, 3 ds, cl r, turn, ¼ inch space. R, 3 ds, p, 3 ds, cl r. Repeat from * once, turn, ¼ inch space. R, 3 ds, join to p of next small r, 3 ds, cl r, turn, ¼ inch space. R, 10 ds, p, 10 ds, cl r, turn, ¼ inch space. R, 10 ds, join to p of next large r, 10 ds, cl r, * turn, ¼ inch space. R, 3 ds, p, 3 ds, cl r, turn, ¼ inch space. R, 3 ds, join to p of next small r, 3 ds, cl r. Repeat from * 3 times, turn, ¼ inch space. R, 3 ds, p, 3 ds, cl r, turn, ¼ inch space. R, 10 ds, join to p of next large r, 10 ds, cl r and complete round to correspond, tie and cut. 8th ROUND: R, 10 ds, join to p of large r, 10 ds, cl r, turn, ¼ inch space. R, 10 ds, p, 10 ds, cl r, turn, ¼ inch space. R, 3 ds, join to p of next small r, 3 ds, cl r, turn, ¼ inch space. R, 3 ds, p, 3 ds, cl r, turn, ¼ inch space. R, 3 ds, join to p of next small r, 3 ds, cl r, turn, ¼ inch space. R, 10 ds, p, 10 ds,

cl r, turn, ¼ inch space. R, 10 ds, join to p of next large r, 10 ds, cl r, * turn, ¼ inch space. R, 3 ds, p, 3 ds, cl r, turn, ¼ inch space. R, 3 ds, join to p of next small r, 3 ds, cl r. Repeat from * 4 times, turn, ¼ inch space. R, 3 ds, p, 3 ds, cl r, turn, ¼ inch space. R, 10 ds, join to p of next large r, 10 ds, cl r, and complete round to correspond, tie and cut. 9th ROUND: R, 10 ds, join to p of large r, 10 ds, cl r, ** turn, ¼ inch space. R, 10 ds, p, 10 ds, cl r, turn, ¼ inch space. R, 3 ds, join to p of small r, 3 ds, cl r, turn, ¼ inch space. R, 10 ds, p, 10 ds, cl r, turn, ¼ inch space. R, 10 ds, join to p of next large r, 10 ds, cl r, * turn, ¼ inch space. R, 3 ds, p, 3 ds, cl r, turn, ¼ inch space. R, 3 ds, join to p of next small r, 3 ds, cl r. Repeat from * 5 times, turn, ¼ inch space. R, 3 ds, p, 3 ds, cl r, turn, ¼ inch space. R, 10 ds, join to p of next large r, 10 ds, cl r. Repeat from ** all around ending to correspond, tie and cut. 10th ROUND: R, 10 ds, join to p of large r, 4 ds, join to p of next large r, 10 ds, cl r, turn, * ¼ inch space. R, 3 ds, p, 3 ds, cl r, turn, ¼ inch space. R, 3ds, join to p of next small r, 3 ds, cl r. Repeat from * 6 times, turn, ¼ inch space. R, 3 ds, p, 3 ds, cl r, turn, ¼ inch space. Repeat from beginning all around, tie and cut. 11th ROUND: R, 5 ds, p, 6 ds, join to p of any small r, 6 ds, p, 5 ds, cl r, turn, ¼ inch space. R, 5 ds, 3 p sep by 6 ds, 5 ds, cl r, turn, ¼ inch space. R, 5 ds, join to corresponding p of 1st r, 6 ds, 2 p sep by 6 ds, 5 ds, cl r, turn, ¼ inch space. R, 5 ds, join to corresponding p of 2nd r, 6 ds, 2 p sep by 6 ds, 5 ds, cl r, turn, ¼ inch space. R, 5 ds, join to p of 3rd r, 6 ds, join to p of next small r, 6 ds, p, 5 ds, cl r, turn, ¼ inch space and complete round to correspond, join, tie and cut.

Spiderweb Dresser Set

Continued from page 13

first r, 8 ds, cl ; repeat from * once more—end made. Work long side as follows :—
** Rw, ch of 6 ds, p, 6 ds. Rw, r of 8 ds, p, 8 ds, cl ; repeat from ** 9 times more. Rw, ch of 6 ds, p, 6 ds. Make other end as follows :—Rw, r of 8 ds, 1 p, 8 ds, cl. (Rw, ch of 4 ds, p, 4 ds, p, 4 ds, rw, r of 8 ds, join to 1 p of this end r, 8 ds, cl) twice. Work along opposite side as follows:—Rw, ch of 6 ds, p, 6 ds. Rw, r of 8 ds, join to corresponding p on long side of oval, 8 ds, cl. Continue thus across, joining last ch to base of first r. Tie and cut.

2nd Row : R of 8 ds, join to first p on first ch of previous row, 8 ds, cl. Rw, ch of (4 ds, p) twice, 4 ds. Rw, r of 8 ds, join to next p on same ch, 8 ds, cl. Rw, ch of (4 ds, p) twice, 4 ds. Rw, r of 8 ds, join to first p on next ch, 8 ds, cl. Rw, ch of (4 ds, p) twice, 4 ds. Rw, r of 8 ds, join to next p on same ch, 8 ds, cl—end completed. * Rw, ch

of 6 ds, p, 6 ds. Rw, r of 8 ds, join to p on next ch, 8 ds, cl ; repeat from * across to opposite end. Work other end and opposite side to correspond, joining last ch to base of first r. Tie and cut.

3rd Row : R of 8 ds, join to p on last ch of previous row, 8 ds, cl. * Rw, ch of (6 ds, p) twice, 6 ds. Rw, r of 8 ds, join to free p, 8 ds, cl ; repeat from * 6 times more—end completed. ** Rw, ch of 8 ds, p, 8 ds. Rw, r of 8 ds, join to next p on previous row, 8 ds, cl ; repeat from ** across. Then work other end and opposite side to correspond, joining last ch to base of first r. Tie and cut.

4th Row : As 3rd row of round doily.

5th to 12th Row : As 4th row of round doily.

13th Row : As 10th row of round doily. Starch and press

Proud Beauty

MATERIALS:

CLARK'S O.N.T. or J. & P. COATS BEST SIX CORD MERCERIZED CROCHET, size 50, 1 ball of White, Ecru, or any color.

Completed doily measures about 9 inches in diameter.

Use shuttle and ball of thread.

First Motif . . . R of 12 ds, p, 12 ds, cl. Ch of 20 ds. Join with shuttle thread to p of r, p, 20 ds. Join to base of r (double r made). Ch of 4 ds, 6 p's sep. by 4 ds, 4 ds, join with shuttle thread to p of double r. Make a center r of 6 ds, 3 p's sep. by 6 ds, 6 ds, cl. * Ch of 4 ds, 6 p's sep. by 4 ds, 4 ds, join to base of double r (p-ring made around double r). Rw, ch of 4 ds, 7 p's sep. by 4 ds, 4 ds. Rw, sr of 4 ds, skip 3 p's of p-ring, join to next p, 4 ds, p, 4 ds, p, 4 ds, cl. Rw, ch

of 4 ds, 7 p's sep. by 4 ds, 4 ds. Rw and make a double r as before. Ch of 4 ds, 3 p's sep. by 4 ds, 4 ds, join to adjacent p of sr, 4 ds, p, 4 ds, p, 4 ds, join with shuttle thread to p of double r. Center-r of 6 ds, p, 6 ds, join to center p of 1st center r, 6 ds, p, 6 ds, cl. Repeat from * until there are 4 sr's, joining last sr to 4th p from base of 1st p-ring and joining last ch to base of 1st p-ring. Tie and cut.

Second Motif . . . Same as 1st motif until 1st sr has been made. Rw, ch of 4 ds, p, 4 ds, p, 4 ds, join to corresponding p of 1st motif, 4 ds, join to next p of 1st motif, 4 ds, 3 p's sep. by 4 ds, 4 ds. Rw and continue working 2nd motif same as 1st motif (no more joinings). Tie and cut.

Third Motif . . . Same as 1st motif until 1st sr has been made. Rw, ch of 4 ds, p,

4 ds, p, 4 ds, skip 2 p-ch's after joining of 1st and second motifs (the ch's on both sides of next sr), join to corresponding p of next p-ch, 4 ds, p, 4 ds, 3 p's sep. by 4 ds, 4 ds. Finish same as 2nd motif. Tie and cut. Make 5 more motifs joining them as 3rd motif was joined to 2nd. Join ch of last motif to corresponding ch of 1st motif. There are now 2 free p-ch's on inner edge of each motif and 4 free p-ch's on outer edge of each motif.

SCALLOPS . . . Pick up joined motifs and work scallops on 2 center free p-ch's of outer edge of each motif (the ch's on both sides of sr opposite inner edge) as follows: Make a double r. Ch of 4 ds, skip 1 p from designated sr of any motif, join to next p, 4 ds. Lr of 5 ds, skip 1 p of same ch of motif, join to next p, 5 ds,

Continued on page 24

Leaf Fantasy

MATERIALS:

CLARK'S O.N.T. or J. & P. COATS BEST SIX CORD MERCERIZED CROCHET, size 30.

CLARK'S O.N.T.—2 balls of White or Ecru, or 3 balls of any color,

OR

J. & P. COATS   —2 balls of White, Ecru or any color.

Completed doily measures about 10½ inches long, by 9½ inches wide.

Use shuttle and ball of thread.

Starting at point, work * r of 14 ds, p, 14 ds, cl. Ch of 3 ds, 5 p's sep. by 3 ds, 3 ds, join to p of r, ch of 6 p's sep. by 3 ds, 3 ds, join to base of r (double r made). Rw, ch of 8 ds, p, 8 ds. Rw. Repeat from * until there are 15 double r's. Rw, ch of 8 ds, 3 p's sep. by 8 ds, 16 ds, join to last p, (8 ds, join to adjacent p) twice; 8 ds, join to base of r, 8 ds, join to next p. ** Rw, make a double r as before, join to same p. Rw, ch of 8 ds, join to base of next r, 8 ds. Repeat from ** until there are 14 double r's. Rw, ch of 8 ds, join to base of 1st r. Tie and cut. **2nd row:** Starting at stem end work along side that has 15 double r's as follows: R of 14 ds, p, 14 ds, cl. Ch of 3 ds, 5 p's sep. by 3 ds, 3 ds, join to p of r, ch of p, 3 ds, join to 5th p from stem, 3 ds, 4 p's sep. by 3 ds, 3 ds, join to base of r. Tie and cut. * R of 14 ds, p, 14 ds, cl. Ch of 3 ds, 4 p's sep. by 3 ds, 3 ds, skip 1 p of same double r on 1st row, join to next p, 3 ds, join to p of r, ch of p, 3 ds, join to 5th p of next double r on 1st row, 3 ds, 4 p's sep. by 3 ds, 3 ds, join to base of r. Tie and cut. Repeat from * across row until there are 15 double r's.

3rd row: Starting at stem end work r of 14 ds, p, 14 ds, cl. Ch of 3 ds, 4 p's sep. by 3 ds, 3 ds, join to last p made on 1st double r of previous row, 3 ds, join to p of r, ch of p, 3 ds, join to 1st p of next double r of previous row, 3 ds, 4 p's sep. by 3 ds, 3 ds, join to base of r. Tie and cut. * R of 14 ds, p, 14 ds, cl. Ch of 3 ds, 4 p's sep. by 3 ds, 3 ds, join to last p of same double r of previous row, 3 ds, join to p of r, ch of p, 3 ds, join to 1st p of next double r of previous row, 3 ds, 4 p's sep. by 3 ds, 3 ds, join to base of r. Tie and cut. Repeat from * across until there are 14 double r's. **4th to 11th rows incl.:** Same as 3rd row but having only 13, 11, 10, 8, 7, 6, 4, and 3 double r's respectively. Work along other side of 1st row as follows: **2nd and 3rd rows:** Starting at stem end, work same as 2nd row of first side until there are 14 double r's. **4th to 11th rows incl.:** Same as 3rd row of first side but having only 12, 11, 9, 8, 7, 5, 4, and 3 double r's respectively.

Scalloped Doily

Materials: Clark's O.N.T. or J. & P. Coats Mercerized Crochet, size 20, 1 ball, 1 shuttle and the ball of thread.

Center medallion: **Make ring of 12 lp's separated by 3 d s. Fasten off securely. * R, 6 d s, join to 1st lp of ring just made, 6 d s, close. Turn work, leave ¼ inch of thread clear, r, 5 d s, 5 p's with 3 d s between, 5 d s, close. Turn work and repeat from * into each lp of 1st ring and joining rings of outer edge. ** Fasten off. Make edging around medallion. R, 6 d s, join to 1st free p of ring on outer edge, 6 d s, close. Turn work, leave ¼ inch of thread clear, r, 5 d s, 5 p's with 3 d s between, 5 d s, close, leave ¼ inch of thread clear and repeat from *, joining next r to 3rd free p on same outer ring of medallion. Continue around medallion, joining 2 inner rings of edging to 1st and 3rd free p's of each outer ring of medallion, and joining together the outer rings of edging.

Make 6 medallions, following directions between **'s for center medallion. Each medallion is joined by center p's of 2 adjacent rings to 2 adjacent rings of center medallion edging. Skip 2 rings of edging between each medallion.

Finishing edge: Tie shuttle and ball thread ends together. **With shuttle thread, r, 5 d s, p, 3 d s, p, 3 d s, join to center p of outer ring of center medallion edging, 3 d s, p, 3 d s, join to center p of adjacent ring, 3 d s, p, 3 d s, p, 5 d s, close. 6 d s ch on ball thread. *R, 6 d s, join to center p of 1st free ring of adjacent medallion, 6 d s, close. On ball thread, make ch of 5 p's with 3 d s between. Repeat from * around edge of medallion, joining to center p of each ring. Repeat from ** joining center of 2nd ch to center p of adjacent ch and continue around doily.

Size 14 x 33

Dainty Dresser Scarf

Materials Required — AMERICAN THREAD COMPANY "STAR" TATTING COTTON.

20 Balls, White or Colors or Shaded, Tinted or Iridescent Colors.

2 Tatting Shuttles.

1st Row. R, 3 d, p, 3 d, p, 3 d, p, 3 d, p, 3 d, close r. R, 3 d, join to last p of last r, 3 d, p, 3 d, p, 3 d, p, 3 d, close r. R, 3 d, join to last p of last r, 3 d, p, 3 d, p, 3 d, close r. Ch, 6 d, p, 3 d, p, 6 d. * R, 3 d, p, 3 d, join to center free p of last r, 3 d, p, 3 d, p, 3 d, close r. R, 3 d. join to last p of last r, 3 d, p, 3 d, p, 3 d, p, 3 d, close r. R, 3 d, join to last p of last r, 3 d, p, 3 d, p, 3 d, p, 3 d, close r. Ch, 6 d, join to last p of last ch, 3 d, p, 6 d, repeat from *. Repeat the three rings joining the first r to last r made and the last r to first ring of motif. Repeat ch joining to last and first ch at picots, break thread and tie ends.

2nd Row. R, 5 p separated by 2 d, close r. Ch 4 d. R, 5 p separated by 2 d, close r. Ch, 6 d, p, 6 d, join to 1st free p of center r of 1st row, 4 d, join to free p of next r, 6 d, p, 6 d. R, 2 d, p, 2 d, p, 2 d, join to center p of last r, 2 d, p, 2 d, p, 2 d, close r. * Ch, 2 d, p, 2 d. R, 2 d, join to last p of last r, 2 d, p, 2 d, p, 2 d, p, 2 d, p, 2 d, close r, repeat from * until there are 7 rings. Ch, 6 d, join to p of last ch of 6 d, 6 d, join to free p of next r in 1st row, 4 d, join to p of next r, 6 d, p, 6 d. R, 2 d, p, 2 d, p, 2 d join to 3rd p of last r, 2 d, p, 2 d, p, 2 d, close r. Ch, 4 d, repeat from beginning all around, break thread and tie ends.

Join motifs together with rings as illustrated. 95 motifs are required. 10 rows of 5 motifs and 10 rows of 4 motifs.

Adventure in Beauty

TATTED DOILY—No. 4502

Materials Required — AMERICAN THREAD COMPANY "STAR" MERCERIZED TATTING COTTON ARTICLE 25

7—60 Yd. Balls White or Colors.

1 Shuttle and 1 Ball.

Center Medallion. R, 3 d, p, 3 d, p, 3 d, p, 3 d, cl r. R, 3 d, join to last p of r, 3 d, p, 3 d, p, 3 d, p, 3 d, cl r. R, 3 d, join to last p of last r, 3 d, p, 3 d, p, 3 d, cl r. R, 3 d, join to last p of last r, 3 d, p, 3 d, p, 3 d, p, 6 d, cl r. Ch, 3 d, p, 3 d, p, 6 d. * R, 3 d, p, 3 d, join to center p of last cluster r, 3 d, p, 3 d, cl r. R, 3 d, join to last p of last r made, 3 d, 4 p sep by 3 d, 3 d cl r. R, 3 d, join to last p of last r made, 3 d, p, 3 d, p, 3 d, cl r. Ch, 3 d, join to p of last ch, 6 d. R, 6 d, join to last p of single r, 3 d, p, 6 d, cl r. Ch, 6 d, p, 3 d. Repeat from * until you have 12 clusters joining the last one to correspond. Break thread and fasten.

2nd Row. * R, 3 d, p, 3 d, join to 1st free p of center r of cluster, 3 d, p, 3 d, cl r. Ch, 6 d, p, 3 d, p, 3 d, p, 6 d. R, 3 d, p, 3 d, join to 3rd p of center r in cluster, 3 d, p, 3 d, cl r. Ch, 6 d, p, 3 d, p, 3 d, p, 6 d. Repeat from * 11 times. Break thread and fasten. Complete each of the next 5 rows in the same manner and start each row in same place.

3rd Row. R, 3 d, p, 3 d, join in 1st p of ch, 3 d, p, 3 d, cl r. Ch, 6 d, p, 3 d, p, 3 d, p, 6 d. R, 3 d, p, join in 3rd p of same ch, 3 d, p, 3 d, cl r. Ch, 6 d, p, 3 d, p, 3 d, p, 6 d. R, 3 d, p, 3 d, join to center p of next ch, 3 d, p, 3 d, cl r. Ch, 6 d, p, 3 d, p, 3 d, p, 6 d. Repeat from beginning all around (36 Rings).

4th, 5th, 6th and 7th Rows are made in the same manner, adding 12 rings in each row.

8th Row. R, 3 d, p, 3 d, p, 3 d, p, 3 d, cl r. Ch, 6 d, p, 3 d, p, 3 d, p, 6 d. R, 6 d, p, 6 d, cl r. Ch, 9 d, join to center p of 1st r, 9 d. R, 6 d, p, 6 d, cl r. Ch, 8 d, p, 8 d. R, 6 d, p, 6 d, cl r. Ch, 7 d, p, 7 d. R, 6 d, p, 6 d, cl r. Ch, 6 d, p, 6 d. R, 6 d, p, 6 d, cl r. Ch, 6 d, p, 6 d. R, 6 d, p, 3 d, p, 3 d, cl r. Ch, 6 d, join to 1st p of initial loop, 3 d, join to 2nd p of same loop, 3 d, join to 3rd p of same loop, 3 d. R, 3 d, join to 3rd p of last r made, 3 d, join to center p of previous r, 3 d, p, 3 d, cl r. Ch, 3 d, join to 1st p of next ch, 3 d, join to 2nd p of same ch, 3 d, join to 3rd p, 6 d. R, 3 d, join to 3rd p of last r made, 3 d, join to center p of 1st r, 6 d, cl r. Ch, 6 d, p, 6 d. R, 6 d, join to corresponding p, 6 d, cl r. Ch, 6 d, p, 6 d. R, 6 d, join to corresponding p, 6 d, cl r. Ch, 7 d, p, 7 d. R, 6 d, join to corresponding p, 6 d, cl r. Ch, 8 d, p, 8 d. R, 6 d, join to corresponding p, 6 d, cl r. Ch, 9 d, p, 9 d. R, 6 d, join to corresponding p, 6 d, cl r. Ch, 6 d, p, 3 d, p, 3 d, p, 6 d. R, 3 d, p, 3 d, join in p of ch 9, 3 d, p, 3 d, cl r. Ch, 6 d, p, 3 d p, 3 d, p, 6 d. R, 6 d, p, 3 d, cl r. Ch, 9 d, join to p of ch 9, 9 d. R, 6 d, p, 6 d, cl r. Ch, 8 d, join to p of ch 8, 8 d, and continue joining ch and r in the same manner all around.

9th Row: R, 3 d, 5 p sep by 3 d, 3 d, cl r. * R, 3 d, join to last p of r, 6 p sep by 3 d, 3 d, cl r. R, 3 d, join to last p of last r, 4 p sep by 3 d, 3 d, cl r. Ch, 6 d. R, 3 d, join to last p of last r, 3 d, p, 3 d, cl r. Ch, 6 d, p, 6 d, p, 4 d, p 6 d, join to 1st p of ch in previous row, 3 d, join to 2nd p of same ch, 3 d, join to 3rd p of same ch, 6 d, p, 4 d. R, 3 d, p, 3 d, join to p between 1st 4 d and 6 d of ch, 3 d, p, 3 d, p, 3 d, cl r. R, 3 d, join to last p of last r, 3 d, join to other p of small r, 3 d, p, 3 d, p, 3 d, p, 3 d, cl r. R, 3 d, join to last p of last r, 3 d, p, 3 d, p, 3 d, p, 3 d, cl r. Ch, 4 d, join to last p of last ch, 6 d, join to the 1st p of next ch in previous row, 3 d, join to 2nd p, 3 d, join to 3rd p of same ch, 6 d, p, 4 d, join to center p of last r made, 6 d, p, 6 d. R, 3 d, join to last free p of 2nd last r leaving 1 p for the center, 3 d, p, 3 d, cl r. Ch, 6 d. R, 3 d, join to p of small r just made, 4 p sep by 3 d, 3 d, cl r, repeat from * all around.

20

Old World Doily

TATTED DOILY 1553

MATERIALS REQUIRED—American Thread Company "Star" Tatting Cotton.

3 Balls—White or Colors.

Each Motif measures about **2** inches—**23** motifs are required for doily, arranged as follows—1 motif at each end. 3 motifs in 2nd and next to the last row and 5 motifs in the 3 center rows. Motifs are joined together at picots as illustrated.

* R, 6 d, p, 3 d, p, 3 d, p, 6 d, close r, R 7 d, p, 4 d, p, 7 d, close r. Repeat from * once, cut and tie thread.
✻ R, 6 d, p, 3 d, p, 3 d, p, 6 d, close r.

R, 7 d, p, 4 d, join to 2nd p of 1st 2 p ring, 7 d, close r. R, 6 d, join to 1st p of 3 p ring, 3 d, p, 3 d, p, 6 d, close R.

R, 7 d, p, 4 d, p, 7 d, close r. Repeat from * until you have 4 sets of 4 rings as illustrated.

Join Shuttle to Ball, * R, 6 d, p, 6 d, join to center p of 3 p small ring, 6 d, p, 6 d, close r.

Ch, 5 d, 7 p separated by 3 d, 5 d. R, 6 d, p 6 d, join to same p as last ring, 6 d, p, 6 d, close r.

Ch, 5 d, 5 p separated by 3 d, 5 d. R, 8 d, join to p of next r, 8 d join to p of next r, 8 d, close r.

Ch, 5 d, 5 p separated by 3 d, 5 d, repeat from * 3 times cut and tie.

Crisp Tatted Doilies

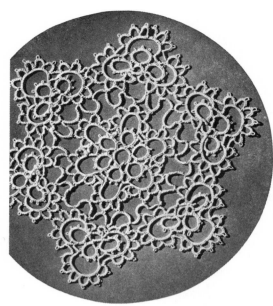

SNOW QUEEN

SNOW QUEEN (left)

. . . Materials: CLARK'S O.N.T. or J. & P. Coats Best Six Cord Mercerized Crochet, size 20, 1 ball of White or Ecru.

Completed doily measures about 7 inches in diameter.

CENTER MOTIF . . . Use two shuttles. **1st rnd:** With 1st shuttle make r of 4 ds, 7 p's sep. by 4 ds, 4 ds, cl. * With thread of 2nd shuttle over left hand, make ch of 5 ds, drop 1st shuttle. With 2nd shuttle make r of 4 ds, join to last p of previous r, 4 ds, 6 p's sep. by 4 ds, 4 ds, cl. Repeat from * 4 more times, joining the 6th r to the first p of the 1st r made. Make ch of 5 ds (as before), join to base of 1st r. Tie and cut.

2nd rnd: Tie threads to 1st free p after a joining of any r of 1st rnd, * ch of 5 ds, 6 p's sep. by 5 ds, 5 ds, join to last free p of same r, ch of 4 ds, join to 1st free p of next r. Repeat from * around, joining last ch to same p where 1st ch was started. Tie and cut. **3rd rnd:** Tie threads to 1st p of any 6-p ch of 2nd rnd. * Ch of 5 ds, p, 5 ds, join to next p of same ch. Repeat from * 4 more times (group of 5 scallops made). Ch of 5 ds, join to 1st p of next 6-p ch. For 2nd group of 5 scallops make ch of 5 ds, join to p of adjacent r, 5 ds, join to next p of the 6-p ch. Ch of 5 ds, p, 5 ds, join to next p of same ch.

Continue in this manner, joining the first ch of each group of 5 scallops to the last p of the previous group, and joining the last ch of the 6th group to the 1st p of the 1st group. When 6th group is completed, make a ch of 5 ds and join to same p where 1st ch was started. Tie and cut.

EDGE MOTIF . . . Using 2 shuttles, work as for center motif until 3 r's are completed. Then make ch of 10 ds, join to base of 1st r. Do not cut threads, but * make a ch of 5 ds, 7 p's sep. by 5 ds, 5 ds, join to last free p of same r, ch of 5 ds, join to 1st free p of next r. Repeat from * 2 more times, joining the 3rd ch to base of 3rd r instead of to a p. Turn work and make scallops around p-chain as follows:

Make ch of 5 ds, p, 5 ds, join to last p on p-ch, ** ch of 5 ds, p, 5 ds, join to p. Repeat from ** 5 more times. Ch of 5 ds, join to first p of next ch. Make a group of 6 scallops on same ch; ch of 5 ds, join to 1st p of next ch—make group of 7 scallops on this ch, joining last scallop to p of 1st scallop and joining end of last scallop to base of r. Make 5 more of these edge motifs, joining to previous edge motif by 4th and 5th scallops. The 6th motif must also be joined to corresponding scallops of first motif.

To Join Edge to Center: Tie threads to 1st free p below joinings between 2 edge motifs. * Ch of 8 ds, join to corresponding p of next edge motif. Rw, ch of 10 ds, join to 1st free p of center motif, 10 ds, join to next p of edge motif, 8 ds, join to next p of center motif, 8 ds, join to next free p of edge motif, 10 ds, join to next p of center motif, 10 ds, join to next p of edge motif. Rw. Repeat from * around, joining last ch to same p where 1st ch was started. Tie and cut.

ROMANCE (below)

. . . Materials: CLARK'S O.N.T. or J. & P. Coats Tatting Cotton, 2 balls.

Completed doily measures about 7 inches in diameter.

CENTER MEDALLION . . . Use shuttle and ball of thread. **1st rnd:** R of 13 ds, lp (3/8-inch high), 13 ds, cl. * Rw, ch of 10 ds, 3 p's sep. by 10 ds, 10 ds. Rw, r of 13 ds, join to lp, 13 ds, cl. Repeat from * 4 more times, make a ch of 10 ds. 3 p's sep. by 10 ds, 10 ds. Join to base of 1st r. Tie ends and cut. **2nd rnd:** R of 5 ds, p, 5 ds, p, 5 ds, join to 3rd p of ch of 1st rnd, 5 ds, cl. * R of 5 ds, join to 1st p of next ch of 1st rnd, 5 ds, p, 5 ds, p, 5 ds, cl. Rw, ch of 10 ds, p, 10 ds, p, 10 ds. Rw, r of 5 ds, p, 5 ds, join to p at center of adjacent r, 5 ds, p, 5 ds, cl.

R of 5 ds, join to last p of preceding r, 5 ds, join to next p of same ch of 1st rnd, 5 ds, p, 5 ds, cl. R of 5 ds, join to p of preceding r, 5 ds, p, 5 ds, p, 5 ds, cl. Rw, ch of 10 ds, p, 10 ds, p, 10 ds. Rw, r of 5 ds, p, 5 ds, join to p at center of preceding r, 5 ds, join to next p of same ch of 1st rnd, 5 ds, cl. Repeat from * around, joining last ch to base of 1st r. Tie ends and cut.

SECOND MEDALLION . . . Work as for center medallion, joining two chains of 2nd rnd to corresponding 4 p's (two on each ch) of center medallion. Tie ends and cut.

Make 5 more medallions same as center medallion, joining chains of 2nd rnd to corresponding p's of center and adjacent medallions.

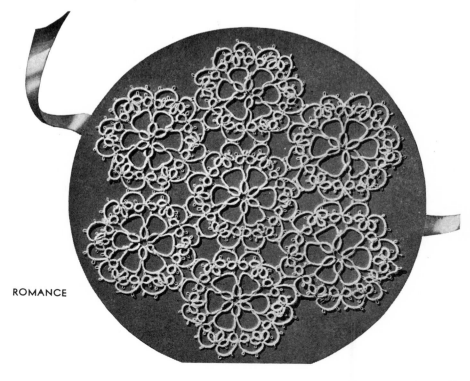

ROMANCE

SNOW SCENE (below)

. . . Materials: CLARK'S O.N.T. or J. & P. COATS BEST SIX CORD MERCERIZED CROCHET, size 50, 1 ball of White, Ecru or any color.

Completed doily measures about 5¼ inches square.

FIRST MOTIF . . . Use shuttle and ball of thread. **1st rnd:** Sr of 4 ds, lp (⅜-inch high), 4 ds, cl. Rw, ch of 7 ds. Rw, lr of 6 ds, 3 p's sep. by 6 ds, 6 ds, cl. * Rw, ch of 7 ds. Rw, sr of 4 ds, join to lp, 4 ds, cl. Rw, ch of 7 ds. Rw, lr of 6 ds, join to next p of last lr, 6 ds, p, 6 ds, p, 6 ds, cl. Repeat from * until there are 12 lr's and 12 sr's, joining last lr to 1st p of 1st lr. Rw, ch of 7 ds, join tightly to base of 1st sr. Tie and cut. **2nd rnd:** Lr of 6 ds, 3 p's sep. by 6 ds, 6 ds, cl. Lr of 6 ds, join to last p of 1st lr, 6 ds, join to free p of lr of 1st rnd, 6 ds, p, 6 ds, cl. Lr of 6 ds, join to last p of last lr, 6 ds, p, 6 ds, p, 6 ds, cl (a clover made).

* Rw, ch of 6 ds, 6 p's sep. by 6 ds, 6 ds. Rw, make a 2nd clover like the 1st, joining 2nd p of 1st r to 2nd p of last r and joining 2nd r to same p of lr of 1st rnd to which 1st clover is joined, also joining 1st p of 3rd r to last p of last r. Rw, ch of 6 ds, p, 6 ds, p, 6 ds. Rw, lr of 6 ds, join to 2nd p of last lr, 6 ds, join to free p of next lr of 1st rnd, 6 ds, p, 6 ds, cl. Rw, ch like last ch. Rw, lr joined to last p of preceding r and to next free p of 1st rnd. Rw, ch like last ch. Rw, clover like 1st clover, joined to last r and to free p of next lr

of 1st rnd. Repeat from * around, tying last side ch to base of 1st clover made.

Make 3 more motifs, joining motifs by 3 p's on each corner ch, and 2 p's on each of the 3 side ch's.

KING WINTER

. . . Materials: CLARK'S O.N.T. or J. & P. COATS BEST SIX CORD MERCERIZED CROCHET, size 50, 1 ball of White, Ecru, or any color.

Completed doily measures about 6 inches in diameter.

CENTER MEDALLION . . . Use shuttle and ball of thread. **1st rnd:** R of 4 ds, lp (⅜-inch high), 4 ds, cl. * Rw, ch of 6 ds, p, 6 ds. Rw, r of 4 ds, join to lp, 4 ds. Repeat from * 4 more times. Rw, ch of 6 ds, p, 6 ds, join to base of 1st r made. Tie ends and cut. **2nd rnd:** * R of 5 ds, join to p of ch of 1st rnd, 5 ds, cl. Rw, short ch of 6 ds, p, 6 ds. Rw, r of 5 ds, join to same p, 5 ds, cl. Rw, long ch of 4 ds, p, 6 ds, p, 4 ds. Rw. Repeat from * around. Join last ch to base of 1st r made. Tie ends and cut.

3rd rnd: * R of 6 ds, join to p of short ch, 6 ds, cl. Rw, ch of 6 ds, p, 6 ds. Rw, r of 6 ds, join to same p, 6 ds, cl. Rw, ch of 5 ds, join to 1st p of long

Continued Below

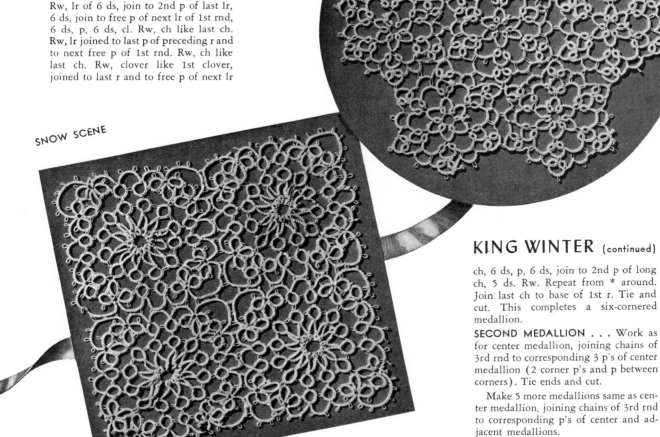

KING WINTER

SNOW SCENE

KING WINTER (continued)

ch, 6 ds, p, 6 ds, join to 2nd p of long ch, 5 ds. Rw. Repeat from * around. Join last ch to base of 1st r. Tie and cut. This completes a six-cornered medallion.

SECOND MEDALLION . . . Work as for center medallion, joining chains of 3rd rnd to corresponding 3 p's of center medallion (2 corner p's and p between corners). Tie ends and cut.

Make 5 more medallions same as center medallion, joining chains of 3rd rnd to corresponding p's of center and adjacent medallions.

Starlight Doily

Shown on page 7

No. 7688

MATERIALS:

J. & P. COATS or CLARK'S O.N.T. BEST SIX CORD MERCERIZED CROCHET, *Size 20,* White or Ecru.

SMALL BALL:

J. & P. COATS —1 ball,

OR

CLARK'S O.N.T.—2 balls.

Starting at center, make r of 1 ds, 12 p's sep. by 2 ds, 1 ds, cl. Tie and cut. **1st row:** Fasten ball and shuttle threads to 1st p of center r, * ch of 5 ds, p, 5 ds, p, 5 ds, skip 1 p and join to next p of center r. Repeat from * around (6 ch's in all). Tie and cut. **2nd row:** Fasten ball and shuttle threads to 1st p of 1st ch of 1st row, * ch of 3 ds, 9 p's sep. by 2 ds, 3 ds and join to 2nd p of same ch. Ch of 3 ds, 3 p's sep. by 2 ds, 3 ds, join to 1st p of next ch. Repeat from * around. Tie and cut. **3rd row:** R of 3 ds, 9 p's sep. by 2 ds, 2 ds, sm p, 3 ds, cl. R of 3 ds, join to sm p of preceding r, 3 ds, 5 p's sep. by 2 ds,

2 ds, join to 2nd p of *short ch* of preceding row, 2 ds, 5 p's sep. by 2 ds, 3 ds, sm p, 3 ds, cl. R of 3 ds, join to sm p of preceding r, 2 ds, 9 p's sep. by 2 ds, 3 ds, cl. Rw, ch of 5 ds, sm p, * 3 ds, 11 p's sep. by 3 ds, 3 ds, sm p, 2 ds. Rw, r of 10 ds, join to 5th p of next *long ch* of preceding row, 10 ds, cl. Rw, ch of 2 ds, join to sm p of preceding ch, 3 ds, 11 p's sep. by 3 ds, 3 ds, sm p, 5 ds. Rw and make another 3-r group as before. Rw, ch of 5 ds, join to sm p of preceding ch and repeat from * around. Tie and cut. **4th row:** * R of 3 ds, 9 p's sep. by 2 ds, 3 ds, cl. Rw, r of 12 ds, join to 6th p of a ch of the preceding row, 12 ds, cl. Ch of 3 ds, 7 p's sep. by 2 ds, 3 ds, join to 9th p of same ch. Ch of 3 ds, p, 3 ds, join to 3rd p of next ch of preceding row. Ch of 3 ds, 7 p's sep. by 2 ds, 3 ds. Repeat from * around. Tie and cut.

5th row: R of 3 ds, 9 p's sep. by 2 ds, 2 ds, sm p, 3 ds, cl. R of 3 ds, join to sm p of preceding r, 3 ds, 11 p's sep. by 2 ds, 3 ds, sm p, 3 ds, cl. R of 3 ds, join to sm p of preceding r, 2 ds, 9 p's sep. by 2 ds, 3 ds, cl. Rw, ch of 5 ds, sm p, 7 ds, join to 7th p of any r on outer edge of pre-

ceding row, 7 ds. * Rw, r of 10 ds, p, 10 ds, cl. Rw, ch of 8 ds, join to 4th p of adjacent *long ch* of preceding row, 8 ds, join to 4th p of *next long ch* of preceding row, 8 ds. Rw, r of 10 ds, join to p of preceding r, 10 ds, cl. Rw, ch of 7 ds, join to 3rd p of next r of preceding row, 7 ds, sm p, 5 ds. Rw, make another 3-r group as before. Rw, ch of 5 ds, join to sm p of preceding ch, 7 ds, join to 7th p of same r. Repeat from * around. Tie and cut. **6th row:** Join ball and shuttle threads to joining-p between group of 2 r's. * Ch of 3 ds, 7 p's sep. by 2 ds, 3 ds, join to 5th p of 1st r of next 3-r group. Ch of 3 ds, 7 p's sep. by 2 ds, 3 ds, join to 3rd p of next r of that group. Ch of 3 ds, 5 p's sep. by 2 ds, 2 ds, sm p, 1 ds. Rw, r of 5 ds, join to 6th p of same r, 5 ds, cl. Rw, r of 1 ds, join to sm p of preceding ch, 2 ds, 7 p's sep. by 2 ds, 2 ds, sm p, 1 ds, cl. Ch of 1 ds, join to sm p of preceding r, 2 ds, 5 p's sep. by 2 ds, 3 ds, join to 9th p of same r of 3-r group. Ch of 3 ds, 7 p's sep. by 2 ds, 3 ds, join to 5th p of 3rd r of same group. Ch of 3 ds, 7 p's sep. by 2 ds, 3 ds, join to joining-p of 2-r group. Repeat from * around. Tie and cut.

Sunburst

Continued from page 11

p, 5 ds, cl. Rw, ch of 5 ds, join to p of adjacent ch, 5 ds. Rw, r of 4 ds, join to adjacent p of previous r, 4 ds, p, 4 ds, p, 4 ds, cl. Rw, ch of 4 ds, join to p of adjacent ch, 4 ds, join to base of 1st ring. Tie and cut.

Second Point . . . R of 3 ds, 3 p's sep. by 3 ds, 3 ds, cl. R of 3 ds, join to adjacent p of previous r, 3 ds, join to next free p of 2nd rnd (to right of previous joining), 3 ds, p, 3 ds, cl. R of 3 ds, join to adjacent p of previous r, 3 ds, join to p of adjacent r of previous point,

3 ds, p, 3 ds, cl. Continue working 2nd point same as 1st point, joining the next 3 r's to adjacent r's of previous point. Finish as for 1st point. Tie and cut. Make 14 more points same as 2nd point, joining 4 r's of last point to adjacent 4 r's of 1st point. Tie and cut.

Proud Beauty

Continued from page 16

3 p's sep. by 5 ds, 5 ds, cl. Ch of 4 ds, 4 p's sep. by 4 ds, 4 ds, join with shuttle thread to p of double r. Ch of p, 4 ds, 4 p's sep. by 4 ds, 4 ds. Lr of 5 ds, 3 p's sep. by 5 ds, 5 ds, join to 4th p from sr on adjacent ch, 5 ds, cl. Ch of 4 ds, skip 1 p of same ch, join to next p (2nd p from sr), 4 ds, join to base of double r. Tie and cut.

CENTER . . . 1st rnd: R of 3 ds, 7 p's

sep. by 3 ds, 3 ds, cl. **2nd rnd:** Ch of sm p, 5 ds, join with shuttle thread to 1st p of r, * ch of p, 5 ds, join with shuttle thread to next p of r. Repeat from * 5 more times. Ch of p, 5 ds, join with shuttle thread to sm p. **3rd rnd:** * Ch of p, 7 ds, join with shuttle thread to next p. Repeat from * around (8 loops). **4th rnd:** * Ch of p, 9 ds, join with shuttle thread to next p. Repeat from * around. Continue in this manner, working 2 more ds on each ch on each rnd. Be careful when joining to adjust shuttle

thread so that all loops on same rnd are even, and work lies perfectly flat. Continue thus until there are 18 rnds in all with 37 ds in each loop. **Next rnd:** Ch of 11 ds, join to 4th p to left of sr on inner edge of any motif, 4 ds, join to next p on motif (3rd p from sr), 11 ds, join to 3rd p of next ch on motif, 4 ds, join to next p of same ch, 11 ds, join to next p of center. Continue in this manner around, joining each ch to one motif of border. Join last ch to beginning of 1st ch. Tie and cut.

BABY GIFTS, COLLARS AND OTHER ACCESSORIES

Portrait Collar and Cuffs

. . . Materials: CLARK'S O.N.T. BEST SIX CORD MERCERIZED CROCHET, size 30, 2 balls of White or Ecru, or 3 balls of any color.

OR

J. & P. COATS BEST SIX CORD MERCERIZED CROCHET, size 30, 2 balls of White, Ecru or any color.

COLLAR . . . Use shuttle and ball of thread. **Fill-in Motifs (Make 2)** . . . R of 3 ds, 3 p's sep. by 3 ds, 3 ds, cl. Rw, ch of 8 ds, p, 4 ds, p, 4 ds. * Rw, r of 3 ds, 3 p's sep. by 3 ds, 3 ds, cl.

Rw, ch of 4 ds, 3 p's sep. by 4 ds, 4 ds. Repeat from * 2 more times. Mark the last p made as p of turning ch to which outer edge of collar is joined later. Continue to work outside edge of fill-in motif as follows: Rw, r of 3 ds, p, 3 ds, join to center p of previous r, 3 ds, p, 3 ds, cl. ** Rw, ch of 4 ds, 3 p's sep. by 4 ds, 4 ds. Rw, r of 3 ds, p, 3 ds, join to center p of opposite r, 3 ds, p, 3 ds, cl. Repeat from ** once more.

Rw, ch of 4 ds, 3 p's sep. by 4 ds, 4 ds. Rw, r of 3 ds, p, 3 ds, join to

center p of 1st r made, 3 ds, p, 3 ds, cl. This completes one half of fill-in motif. Rw, ch of 4 ds, 3 p's sep. by 4 ds, 4 ds. Rw. For second half make r of 3 ds, p, 3 ds, join to same p as previous r, 3 ds, p, 3 ds, cl. Continue around, making second half same as first. After last r make ch of 4 ds, p, 4 ds, join to opposite p of 1st ch, 8 ds, join to base of 1st r. Tie and cut. Mark corresponding p of 2nd turning ch in same manner as on other side.

Continued on page 46

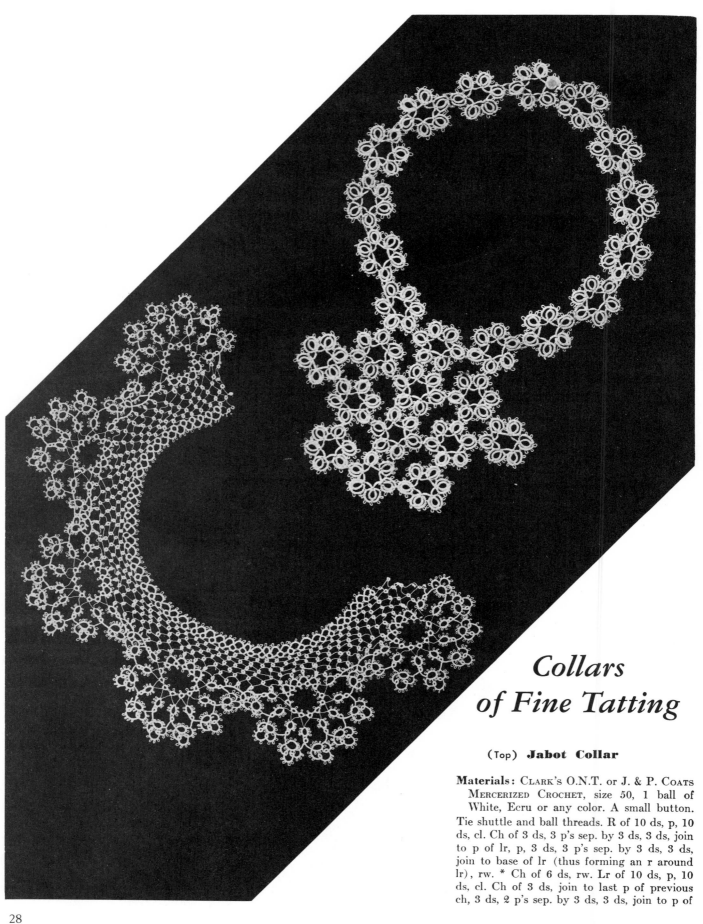

Collars of Fine Tatting

(Top) **Jabot Collar**

Materials: CLARK'S O.N.T. or J. & P. COATS
MERCERIZED CROCHET, size 50, 1 ball of
White, Ecru or any color. A small button.

Tie shuttle and ball threads. R of 10 ds, p, 10
ds, cl. Ch of 3 ds, 3 p's sep. by 3 ds, 3 ds, join
to p of lr, p, 3 ds, 3 p's sep. by 3 ds, 3 ds,
join to base of lr (thus forming an r around
lr), rw. * Ch of 6 ds, rw. Lr of 10 ds, p, 10
ds, cl. Ch of 3 ds, join to last p of previous
ch, 3 ds, 2 p's sep. by 3 ds, 3 ds, join to p of

lr, p, 3 ds, 3 p's sep. by 3 ds, 3 ds, join to base of lr, rw. Repeat from * until 6 double r's are made, taking care to join the ch around last r at both sides. Join last ch at base of 1st r. This completes 1 motif. Make another motif, joining center p of 1 r to center p of adjacent r of 1st motif. Make another motif, joining in same manner to opposite side of 1st motif. Make 12 more motifs to go around neck edge, 6 motifs on each side of previous ones, joining with 3 p's instead of 1 p (opening is center back).

JABOT . . . Make 3 motifs and join to the center 3 motifs of neck piece as those motifs were joined (1 p joined). Make 3 more motifs and join to last 3 motifs (1 p joined). Make another motif and join between the 2 rows of 3 motifs, joining center p of outside r to center p of outside r on 2nd row, and joining center p of next r to center p of adjacent r of 1st row. Finish other side the same. Make 3 more motifs, joining to center 3 motifs as before. Fasten at back of neck with button and a loop.

Circular Collar

Shown on page 28, bottom

Materials: CLARK'S O.N.T. or J. & P. COATS TATTING COTTON, 2 balls.

FIRST MOTIF . . . Tie shuttle and ball threads. Sr of 5 ds, 3 p's sep. by 3 ds, 5 ds, cl. * Rw, ch of 5 ds, 3 p's sep. by 3 ds, 5 ds, sr of 5 ds, join to last p of previous r, 3 ds, p, 3 ds, p, 5 ds, cl. Repeat from * 2 more times. Rw, ch of 5 ds, 3 p's sep. by 3 ds, 5 ds. Tie ends and cut away ball thread. ** Make another sr, joining as before. Rw, sp (⅜-inch). Lr of 3 ds, 8 p's sep. by 3 ds, 3 ds, cl. Rw, sp. Repeat from ** until 8 lr's and 12 sr's are made, joining the last sr to 1st sr. Join to base of 1st sr. Tie and cut. Make 5 more motifs like this.

OUTER EDGE OF MOTIFS . . . Tie threads. Ch of 1 ds, p, 7 ds, rw. Sr of 4 ds, skip 1 p of 1st lr, join to next p, 3 ds, join to next p of same lr, 4 ds, cl. Rw, ch of 7 ds. Rw, lr of 3 ds, 10 p's sep. by 3 ds, 3 ds, cl. Rw, ch of 4 ds, 3 p's sep. by 3 ds, 4 ds, skip 1 p of lr, join to next p, ch like last ch, skip 1 p, join to next p, ch like last, skip 1 p, join to next p. * Ch of 7 ds, rw. Sr like 1st, joined to next lr of motif as before. Rw, ch of 7 ds. Rw, lr like previous lr. Rw, ch of 4 ds, 3 p's sep. by 3 ds, 4 ds. Rw, sr of 5 ds, join to 2nd p of lr, 5 ds, cl. Rw, ch of 4 ds, 3 p's sep. by 3 ds, 4 ds. Rw, sr like previous one, joining to 4th p. Rw, ch of 4 ds, 3 p's sep. by 3 ds, 4 ds, join to 6th p. Repeat from * 5 more times. Ch of 7 ds, rw. Sr, joined to next lr as before. Rw, ch of 4 ds, 4 p's sep. by 4 ds, 4 ds. Rw, r of 5 ds, join

Continued on page 31

Petal Point Collar and Cuff Set

Materials: CLARK'S O.N.T. or J. & P. COATS MERCERIZED CROCHET, size 30, 2 balls of White, Ecru, or any color.

COLLAR . . . **1st row:** R of 4 ds, 3 p's sep. by 4 ds, 4 ds, cl. Rw, sp (⅛-inch). R of 3 ds, 3 p's sep. by 3 ds, 3 ds, cl. * Rw, sp. R of 4 ds, join to last p of adjacent r, 4 ds, p, 4 ds, p, 4 ds, cl. Rw, sp. R of 3 ds, join to last p of adjacent r, 3 ds, p, 3 ds, p, 3 ds, cl. Repeat from * until 76 sr's and 77 lr's are made. Tie ends and cut. **2nd row:** Tie shuttle and ball threads. R of 4 ds, p, 4 ds, join to center p of lr on 1st row, 4 ds, p, 4 ds, cl. * Rw, ch of 7 ds, p, 7 ds. Rw, r of 4 ds, p, 4 ds, skip 1 r, join to center p of next r, 4 ds, p, 4 ds, cl. Repeat from *

until 39 r's and 38 ch's are made; turn. **3rd row:** Ch of 4 ds, 3 p's sep. by 4 ds, 4 ds. * Rw, r of 4 ds, p, 4 ds, join to p of next ch on 2nd row, 4 ds, p, 4 ds, cl. Rw, ch of 4 ds, 3 p's sep. by 4 ds, 4 ds. Repeat from * until 38 r's and 39 ch's are made. Rw, ch of 4 ds, 3 p's sep. by 4 ds, 4 ds, join to base of last r. Tie ends and cut. **4th row:** R of 3 ds, p, 3 ds, join to 3rd p of 1st ch on 3rd row, 3 ds, p, 3 ds, cl. Rw, sp (⅛-inch). R of 4 ds, 3 p's sep. by 4 ds, 4 ds, cl. * Rw, sp; r of 3 ds, join to last p of adjacent r, 3 ds, join to next p of next ch on 3rd row, 3 ds, p, 3 ds, cl. Rw, sp, r of 4 ds, join to last p of adjacent r, 4 ds, 2 p's sep. by 4 ds, 4 ds, cl. Repeat from * until 114 sr's and 113 lr's are made. Tie ends and cut. **5th row:** Tie threads. R

Continued on page 45

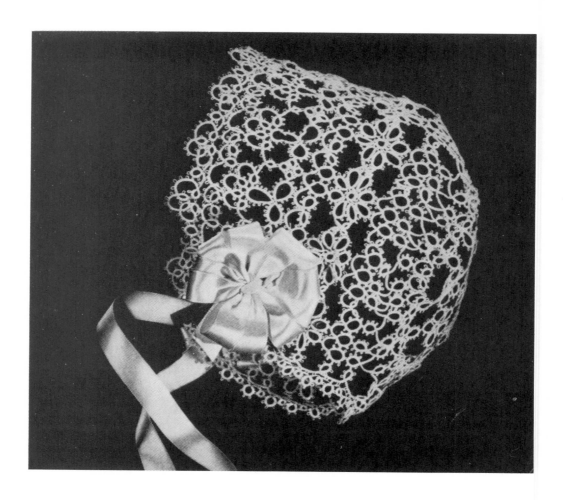

Exquisite Baby Cap

No. 5042 Materials: Clark's O.N.T. or J. & P. Coats Mercerized Crochet, size 50, 2 balls of White.

2 rosettes and 1 yd. ribbon, ½ inch wide.

CROWN . . . **Center Daisy.** Use one shuttle. Center r of 1 ds, 6 p's sep. by 2 ds, 1 ds. Tie, but do not cut. R of 7 ds, 3 p's sep. by 7 ds, 7 ds, cl. * Join to nearest p of center r. R of 7 ds, join to last p of last r, 7 ds, p, 7 ds, p, 7 ds, cl. Repeat from * around, joining 6th r to 1st one. Tie and cut. **1st rnd:** Make center r as before and, after each r is drawn up, join to nearest p of center r. R of 7 ds, 7 p's sep. by 3 ds, 7 ds, cl. R of 7 ds, join to last p of last r, 3 ds, 6 p's sep. by 3 ds, 7 ds, cl. When working next ring, join it to a r of the daisy thus: R of 7 ds, join to last p of last r, 3 ds, p, 3 ds, p, 3 ds, join to center p of r of center daisy, 3 ds, 3 p's sep. by 3 ds, 7 ds, cl. R of 7 ds, join to last p of last r, 3 ds, 6 p's sep. by 3 ds, 7 ds, cl. Make 2 more similar r's, joining last p

of 6th r to 1st p of 1st r. Finish off as before. Make 5 more daisies like this, joining to center daisy in same way and joining to each other by the next r's after joining to center daisy. **2nd rnd:** Tie shuttle and ball threads. R of 4 ds, 5 p's sep. by 4 ds, 4 ds, cl. * Rw, ch of 3 ds, 5 p's sep. by 3 ds, 3 ds (make all ch's of this rnd like this ch). *Now make a clover leaf as follows:* 1st ring of 3 ds, p, 3 ds, p, 3 ds, join to 2nd last p of last r, 3 ds, p, 3 ds, p, 3 ds, cl. 2nd ring of 3 ds, join to last p of 1st ring, 3 ds, 3 p's sep. by 3 ds, 3 ds, join to center p of 1st r on outer edge of a daisy, 3 ds, 4 p's sep. by 3 ds, 3 ds, cl. 3rd ring of 3 ds, join to last p of 2nd ring, 3 ds, 4 p's sep. by 3 ds, 3 ds, cl. Rw, ch as before. R of 4 ds, join to 3rd p of last r, 4 ds, p, 4 ds, cl. Rw, ch as before. R of 3 ds, p, 3 ds, p, 3 ds, join to p of last r, 3 ds, p, 3 ds, p, 3 ds, cl. Close beside make another r of 3 ds, 5 p's sep. by 3 ds, 3 ds, cl. Rw, ch as before. R of 4 ds, join to 3rd p of last r, 4 ds, p, 4 ds, cl. Rw, ch as before. Make another

clover leaf like last one, joining 1st ring to p of last sr. Join 2nd ring to center of 3rd ring of same daisy. After 3rd ring of clover make the usual chain. Rw, r of 4 ds, p, 4 ds, join to 3rd p of last r, 4 ds, 3 p's sep. by 4 ds, 4 ds, cl. Repeat from * around, and finish off rnd securely. **3rd rnd:** * R of 3 ds, 3 p's sep. by 3 ds, 3 ds, join to 3rd p of a ch of last rnd, 3 ds, 3 p's sep. by 3 ds, 3 ds, cl, rw. Ch of 10 ds, rw. R of 8 ds, 7 p's sep. by 3 ds, 3 ds, cl. Rw, ch of 10 ds. Rw, repeat from * around. Work is now done in rows instead of rnds. **1st row:** R of 4 ds, 3 p's sep. by 4 ds, 4 ds, join to 4th p of a r of last rnd, 4 ds, 3 p's sep. by 4 ds, 4 ds, cl. * Rw, ch of 4 ds, 3 p's sep. by 4 ds, 4 ds. Rw, r of 4 ds, p, 4 ds, join to 2nd last p of last r, 4 ds, p, 4 ds, join to 4th p of next r of last rnd, 4 ds, 3 p's sep. by 4 ds, 4 ds, cl. Rw, ch same as last ch. Rw, r same as last r. Rw, ch of 3 ds, 3 p's sep. by 3 ds, 3 ds. R of 5 ds, join to 2nd last p of last r, 5 ds, cl. Close beside make another r of 5 ds, p, 5 ds, cl. Rw, ch same as last ch. Rw, r of 4 ds, p, 4 ds, join to p of last r, 4 ds, p, 4 ds, join to 4th p of next r of last rnd, 4 ds, 3 p's sep. by 4 ds, 4 ds, cl. Repeat from * until there are 11 groups of 3 lr's. Tie and cut. **2nd row:** There are 11 daisies in this row. They are worked exactly the same as those of the 1st rnd. Join each daisy by 2 of its r's to 2nd p's of the ch's above the 3 r's in each group of last row. Do not join daisies, but connect them with four-leaf clovers as follows: R of 5 ds, join to 3rd p of a r on side of a daisy, 5 ds, cl. Work 3 more r's like this, joining next r to 3rd p of next r, and the following 2 r's to 3rd p's of adjacent 2 r's of next daisy. Tie tightly in the center. **3rd row:** R of 4 ds, 3 p's sep. by 4 ds, 4 ds, join to 3rd p of 3rd r, counting from 1st joining of 1st daisy on last row, 4 ds, 3 p's sep. by 4 ds, 4 ds, cl. * Rw, ch of 4 ds, 3 p's sep. by 4 ds, 4 ds. Rw, r of 4 ds, p, 4 ds, join to 2nd last p of last r, 4 ds, p, 4 ds, join to 3rd p of next r of daisy, 4 ds, 3 p's sep. by 4 ds, 4 ds, cl. Rw, ch of 3 ds, 5 p's sep. by 3 ds, 3 ds. R of 3 ds, 3 p's sep. by 3 ds, 3 ds, join to 2nd last p of last r, 3 ds, 3 p's sep. by 3 ds, 3 ds, cl. Close beside make another r of 3 ds, 7 p's sep. by 3 ds, 3 ds, cl. Rw, ch as last ch. R of 4 ds, p, 4 ds, join to 4th p of last r, 4 ds, p, 4 ds, join to 3rd p of 1st r of next daisy, 4 ds, 3 p's sep. by 4 ds, 4 ds, cl. Repeat from * around, ending to correspond with beginning. **4th row:** This row is of large three-leaf clovers, and small four-leaf clovers.

Make four-leaf clover as follows: 1st ring of 4 ds, 3 p's sep. by 4 ds, 4 ds, cl. 2nd ring of 4 ds, join to 3rd p of 1st ring, 4 ds, p, 4 ds, p, 4 ds, cl. 3rd ring of 4 ds, join to last p of 2nd ring, 4 ds, join to 2nd p of 1st ch of last row, 4 ds, p, 4 ds, cl. 4th ring like 2nd, but join last p to 1st p of 1st ring. Tie and cut.

Make three-leaf clover as follows: 1st ring of 3 ds, p, 3 ds, p, 3 ds, join to 3rd p of next 5-p ch of last row, 3 ds, 3 p's sep. by 3 ds, 3 ds, join to p of 4th r of small four-leaf clover, 3 ds, 5 p's sep. by 3 ds, 3 ds, cl. 2nd ring of 3 ds, join to last p of 1st ring, 3 ds, 13 p's sep. by 3 ds, 3 ds, cl. 3rd ring of 3 ds, join to last p of 2nd ring, 3 ds, 8 p's sep. by 3 ds, 3 ds, join to 3rd p of next ch of last row, 3 ds, p, 3 ds, p, 3 ds. Tie and cut.

Make next four-leaf clover as follows: 1st ring of 4 ds, 3 p's sep. by 4 ds, 4 ds, cl. 2nd ring of 4 ds, join to last p of 1st ring, 4 ds, join to 5th p of 3rd ring of large clover, 4 ds, p, 4 ds, cl. 3rd ring, join to last p of last r, 4 ds, join to center p of next ch on previous row, 4 ds, p, 4 ds, cl. Make 4th ring as before, joining on both sides. Alternate clovers to end of row. **5th row:** 11 scallops are worked in this row, their r's being joined to 2nd r's of large clovers of last row. Tie threads. R of 3 ds, p, 3 ds, p, 3 ds, join to 5th p of lr of 1st clover of last row, 3 ds, p, 3 ds, p, 3 ds, cl. * Rw, ch of 3 ds, 5 p's sep. by 3 ds, 3 ds. Rw, r of 3 ds, p, 3 ds, join to 2nd last p of last r, 3 ds, join to next p of clover ring, 3 ds, p, 3 ds, p, 3 ds, cl. Work 2 more similar ch's and r's, rw. After 4th r make a ch of 3 ds, p, 3 ds, rw. R of 3 ds, p, 3 ds, join to free p of small four-leaf clover, 3 ds, p, 3 ds, cl. Ch same as last ch. R of 3 ds, p, 3 ds, p, 3 ds, join to 5th p of lr of next clover, 3 ds, p, 3 ds, p, 3 ds, cl. Repeat from * to end of row. Now work in rnds as follows:

1st rnd: This rnd is worked around entire cap. R of 3 ds, p, 3 ds, p, 3 ds, join to 4th p of 1st ch of 1st scallop, 3 ds, p, 3 ds, cl. * Rw, ch of 3 ds, 5 p's sep. by 3 ds, 3 ds, rw. R of 3 ds, p, 3 ds, p, 3 ds, join to 2nd p of 3rd ch of same scallop, 3 ds, p, 3 ds, p, 3 ds, cl. Rw, ch of 3 ds, 3 p's sep. by 3 ds, 3 ds, rw.

R of 3 ds, p, 3 ds, p, 3 ds, join to 2nd last p of last r, 3 ds, p, 3 ds, p, 3 ds, cl. Close beside make another r of 3 ds, 5 p's sep. by 3 ds, 3 ds, cl. Rw, ch same as last ch. Rw, r of 3 ds, p, 3 ds, join to 3rd p of last r, 3 ds, join to 4th p of 1st ch of next scallop, 3 ds, p, 3 ds, p, 3 ds, cl. Repeat from * to end of rnd. After the last r, make another ch with 5 p's. Work another r like last r, joining it to 4th p of 3rd ch of end scallop. Now work along the neck edge of cap, making all ch's of 3 ds, 3 p's sep. by 3 ds, 3 ds, and all r's similar to last r. Join them to center p's of r's to draw cap into shape. **2nd rnd:** The edging along front of cap is worked in this rnd. R of 4 ds, join to 2nd p of 1st of a pair of ch's with only 1 p on them, 4 ds, p, 1 ds, p, 4 ds, p, 4 ds, cl. Rw, ch of 3 ds, 4 p's sep. by 3 ds, 3 ds. * Rw, r of 4 ds, p, 4 ds, join to 2nd p in center of last r, 1 ds, p, 4 ds, p, 4 ds, cl. Rw, ch of 3 ds, 4 p's sep. by 3 ds, 3 ds. Rw, another r and ch similar to the last. R of 4 ds, p, 4 ds, join to p of last r, 1 ds, join to p in center of 1st r, 4 ds, join to 2nd p of next ch of last rnd, 4 ds, cl. Ch of 4 ds, join to 2nd p of next ch, rw. R of 4 ds, join to 3rd p of 3rd ch of scallop just made, 3 ds, 4 p's sep. by 3 ds, 4 ds, cl. Rw, ch as last ch, joining to 4th p of same ch of last rnd. R same as 1st r of this rnd. Ch of 3 ds, p, 3 ds, join to 4th p of r before the last, 3 ds, 3 p's sep. by 3 ds, 3 ds. Repeat from * to end of front of cap. Tie and cut. Now with shuttle work rings along neck edge as follows: R of 4 ds, join to 4th p of last ch of last scallop at front, 3 ds, 4 p's sep. by 3 ds, 4 ds, cl. Join to a p of ch of last rnd. ** R of 4 ds, join to last p of last r, 4 ds, p, 4 ds, cl. Join to p of ch further along. R of 4 ds, join to p of last r, 3 ds, 4 p's sep. by 3 ds, 4 ds, cl. Join again further along. Repeat from ** across to front edge. Tie and cut. Sew on rosettes and ribbon for ties.

Circular Collar

Continued from page 29

to 3rd p of adjacent ch, 6 ds, join to 1st p of next ch, 6 ds, p, 5 ds, cl. Rw, ch of 4 ds, 4 p's sep. by 4 ds, 4 ds. Rw, sr joined to 1st lr of 2nd motif as before. Rw, ch of 7 ds. Lr of 3 ds, 10 p's sep. by 3 ds, 3 ds, cl. Rw, ch of 4 ds, p, 3 ds, p, 3 ds, join to last p of adjacent r, 4 ds, join to 2nd p of lr, ch of 4 ds, join to p of adjacent ch where r was joined; 3 ds, join to next p, 3 ds, p, 4 ds. Finish edge as for 1st motif. Join all other motifs in same way, ending with ch of 7 ds, p, 1

ds. Tie and cut. Join shuttle to center p of last ch connecting circle of sr's. Sp (3/8-inch), sr of 4 ds, join to 2nd p of next lr, 4 ds, cl. Sp, sr as before, joining to 2nd p of next ch. Sp, sr, joining to 4th p of same ch. Sp, r as before, joining to 2nd p of next ch, another r joined to 4th p of same ch. Sp, r as before, joining to center p of lr. Sp, and tie securely to center p of next connecting ch. Cut thread. Fill in all spaces between motifs and half-spaces at each end in same way. **Next row:** R of 4 ds, join to p of 1st ch made, sp (1/2-inch), sr of 4 ds,

join to center p of lr. * Sp, r of 4 ds, join to center p of next ch, 4 ds, cl. Repeat from * 3 more times. Sp, r of 4 ds, join to next sp. Continue thus across row, ending to correspond with beginning; make r of 8 ds, cl, turn. Repeat the last row 4 more times, graduating the sps in each row to shape collar. Tie shuttle and ball threads. R of 5 ds, p, 5 ds, join to 1st sp, 5 ds, p, 5 ds, cl. ** Rw, ch of 5 ds, 2 p's sep. by 3 ds, 5 ds. Rw, r of 5 ds, join to p of last r, 5 ds, join to next sp, 5 ds, p, 5 ds, cl. Repeat from ** across.

Petals

MATERIALS:

CLARK'S O.N.T. or J. & P. COATS BEST SIX CORD MERCERIZED CROCHET, size 50, 1 ball of White or Ecru.

Use shuttle and ball of thread.

R of 3 ds, 3 p's sep. by 3 ds, 3 ds, cl. Close to this make r of 3 ds, 3 p's sep. by 3 ds, 3 ds, cl. (Rw, ch of 6 ds, p, 6 ds. Rw, r of 3 ds, 3 p's sep. by 3 ds, 3 ds, cl) twice. * Rw, ch of 6 ds, p, 6 ds. Rw, r of 4 ds, p, 4 ds, p, 4 ds, cl. Rw, ch of 6 ds. Rw, r of 4 ds, join to p of adjacent r, 4 ds, p, 4 ds, p, 4 ds, cl. R of 4 ds, join to p of adjacent r, 2 ds, 6 p's sep. by 2 ds, 4 ds, cl. R of 4 ds, join to last p of previous r, 4 ds, p, 4 ds, p, 4 ds, cl. Rw, ch of 6 ds. Rw, r of 4 ds, join to p of adjacent r, 4 ds, p, 4 ds, cl. (Rw, ch of 6 ds, join to p of opposite ch, 6 ds. Rw, r of 3 ds, 3 p's sep. by 3 ds, 3 ds, cl) twice. Rw, ch of 6 ds, join to p of opposite ch, 6 ds. Rw, r of 3 ds, p, 3 ds, join to center p of adjacent r, 3 ds, p, 3 ds, cl. R of 3 ds, 3 p's sep. by 3 ds, 3 ds, cl. (Rw, ch of 6 ds, p, 6 ds. Rw, r of 3 ds, p, 3 ds, join to center p of opposite r, 3 ds, p, 3 ds, cl) twice. Repeat from * for desired length of collar, making end correspond with beginning. Tie and cut.

V-Neck Collar

. . . Materials: CLARK'S O.N.T. OR J. & P. COATS TATTING COTTON, 3 balls.

Use shuttle and ball of thread. **1st row:** R of 5 ds, 3 p's sep. by 4 ds, 5 ds, cl. R of 5 ds, 3 p's sep. by 4 ds, 5 ds, cl. * Rw, ch of 8 ds, p, 8 ds. Rw, r of 5 ds, p, 4 ds, join to center p of previous r, 4 ds, p, 5 ds, cl. R of 5 ds, 3 p's sep. by 4 ds, 5 ds, cl. Repeat from * 16 more times. ** Rw, ch of 8 ds, p, 8 ds. Rw, r of 4 ds, p, 3 ds, join to center p of previous r, 3 ds, p, 4 ds, cl. R of 4 ds, 3 p's sep. by 3 ds, 4 ds, cl. Repeat from ** 11 more times. *** Rw, ch of 8 ds, p, 8 ds. Rw, r of 5 ds, p, 4 ds, join to center p of previous r, 4 ds, p, 5 ds, cl. R of 5 ds, 3 p's sep. by 4 ds, 5 ds, cl. Repeat from *** 17 more times. Tie and cut.

FILL-IN STRIP . . . R of 7 ds, lp, 7 ds, cl. Rw, ch of 4 ds, 3 p's sep. by 4 ds, 4 ds. Rw, r of 7 ds, join to lp, 7 ds, cl. Rw, ch of 4 ds, 6 p's sep. by 2 ds, 4 ds, cl. Rw, r of 7 ds, join to lp, 7 ds, cl. Rw, ch of 4 ds, p, 4 ds, join to p of 1st ch on 1st row, 4 ds, p, 4 ds. Rw, r of 7 ds, join to lp, 7 ds, cl. * Rw, ch of 8 ds, p, 8 ds. Rw, r of 5 ds, p, 4 ds, join to p of next ch of 1st row, 4 ds, p, 5 ds, cl. Repeat from * 7 more times.

Continued on page 45

Pleasure Bent

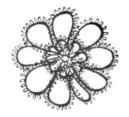

MATERIALS: J. & P. Coats or Clark's O.N.T. Best Six Cord Mercerized Crochet, *Size 30:* **Small Ball:** J. & P. Coats—*3 balls of White or Ecru, or 4 balls of any color, or* Clark's O.N.T.—*5 balls of White or Ecru, or 6 balls of any color.*

COLLAR . . . Use shuttle and ball threads.

FILL-IN MOTIF (Make 2) . . .
R of 3 ds, 3 p's sep by 3 ds, 3 ds, cl. Rw, ch of 8 ds, p, 4 ds, p, 4 ds. * Rw, r of 3 ds, 3 p's sep by 3 ds, 3 ds, cl. Rw, ch of 4 ds, 3 p's sep by 4 ds, 4 ds. Repeat from * 2 more times. Mark the last p made as p of turning chain to which outer edge of collar is joined later. Continue to work outside edge of Fill-in Motif as follows: Rw, r of 3 ds, p, 3 ds, join to center p of previous r, 3 ds, p, 3 ds, cl. ** Rw, ch of 4 ds, 3 p's sep by 4 ds, 4 ds. Rw, r of 3 ds, 3 p's sep by 3 ds, join to center p of opposite r, 3 ds, p, 3 ds, cl. Repeat from ** once more.

Rw, ch of 4 ds, 3 p's sep by 4 ds, 4 ds. Rw, r of 3 ds, p, 3 ds, join to center p of first r made, 3 ds, p, 3 ds, cl. This completes one half of Fill-in Motif. Rw, ch of 4 ds, 3 p's sep by 4 ds, 4 ds. Rw. For second half make r of 3 ds, p, 3 ds, join to same p as previous r, 3 ds, p, 3 ds, cl. Continue around, making second half to correspond with side just completed. After last r make ch of 4 ds, p, 4 ds, join to opposite p of first chain, 8 ds, join to base of first r. Tie and cut. Mark corresponding p of 2nd turning chain in same manner as on other side.

OUTER EDGE OF COLLAR . . .
R of 2 ds, 5 p's sep by 2 ds, 2 ds, cl. * Rw, ch of 3 ds, 3 p's sep by 3 ds, 3 ds. Rw, r of 2 ds, p, 2 ds, skip 1 p of previous r, join to next p, 2 ds, 3 p's sep by 2 ds, 2 ds, cl. Repeat from * once more. Rw, ch of 3 ds, 3 p's sep by 3 ds, 3 ds. R of 2 ds, 5 p's sep by 2 ds, 2 ds, cl. Ch of 3 ds, 3 p's sep by 3 ds, 3 ds. Rw, r of 2 ds, p, 2 ds, join to corresponding p of opposite r, 2 ds, 3 p's sep by 2 ds, 2 ds, cl. Rw, ch of 3 ds, 3 p's sep by 3 ds, 3 ds. Rw, r of 2 ds, p, 2 ds, join to corresponding p of last r, 2 ds, 3 p's sep by 2 ds, 2 ds, cl. Rw, ch of 3 ds, 3 p's sep by 3 ds, 3 ds. Rw, r of 2 ds, p, 2 ds, join to corresponding p of previous r, 2 ds, p, 2 ds, join to corresponding p of first r, 2 ds, p, 2 ds, cl (end motif, or point of Collar completed).

Ch of 4 ds, 3 p's sep by 4 ds, 4 ds. Work next motif as follows: R of 2 ds, 5 p's sep by 2 ds, 2 ds, cl. Rw, ch of 3 ds, p, 3 ds, join to last p of adjacent chain of end motif, 3 ds, p, 3 ds. ** Rw, r of 2 ds, p, 2 ds, join to corresponding p of previous r, 2 ds, 3 p's sep by 2 ds, 2 ds, cl. Rw, ch of 3 ds, 3 p's sep by 3 ds, 3 ds. Repeat from ** 4 more times.

Rw, r of 2 ds, p, 2 ds, join to corresponding p of previous r, 2 ds, p, 2 ds, join to corresponding p of first r of same motif, 2 ds, p, 2 ds, cl (7-r

motif completed). Ch of 4 ds, 3 p's sep by 4 ds, 4 ds. Rw, make a single r of 2 ds, p, 2 ds, join to center p of last chain of previous motif, 2 ds, 3 p's sep by 2 ds, 2 ds, cl. Rw, make adjoining chain of 4 ds, p, 4 ds, join a marked p of turning chain of one Fill-in Motif, 4 ds, p, 4 ds.

Start next 7-r motif as follows: R of 2 ds, 5 p's sep by 2 ds, 2 ds, cl. Rw, ch of 3 ds, p, 3 ds, skip one p of single r, join to next p, 3 ds, p, 3 ds. Continue as for last motif until 7th r is completed. *** Make a joining ch of 4 ds, p, 4 ds, join to center p of next ch of outside edge of Fill-in Motif, 4 ds, p, 4 ds. Rw, make single r, joining to previous motif as before. Rw, make a joining ch of 4 ds, p, 4 ds, join to center p of next ch of Fill-in Motif, 4 ds, p, 4 ds. Make a 7-r motif, joining first ch to last single r as before. Repeat from *** once more. Ch of 4 ds, p, 4 ds, join to same p of Fill-in Motif where last joining ch was joined, 4 ds, p, 4 ds. Rw. Work and join as before the following: a single r, rw, a joining ch, a 7-r motif, a joining ch, rw, a single r, rw, a joining ch, and a 7-r motif. Continue as follows: Ch of 4 ds, p, 4 ds, join to other marked p of Fill-in Motif, 4 ds, p, 4 ds. **** Rw, make a single r, rw, ch of 4 ds, 3 p's sep by 4 ds, 4 ds. Make a 7-r motif, ch of 4 ds, 3 p's sep by 4 ds, 4 ds. Repeat from **** 10 more times. Rw, make a single r. Ch of 4 ds, p, 4 ds, join to marked p of 2nd Fill-in Motif, 4 ds, p, 4 ds. Continue to work as for other

Continued on page 45

Necklace Collar

... Materials: CLARK'S O.N.T. OR J. & P. COATS BEST SIX CORD MERCERIZED CROCHET, size 20, 2 balls of White or Ecru.

FIRST MOTIF ... Use shuttle and ball of thread. Tie ball and shuttle threads. On ball thread make sm p and 1 ds (center p made). Rw, ch of 8 ds. R of 2 ds, 3 p's sep. by 3 ds, 2 ds, cl. Ch of 8 ds, join to center p; ch of 9 ds. R of 3 ds, join to last p of previous r, 4 ds, 2 p's sep. by 4 ds, 3 ds, cl. Ch of 9 ds, join to center p. On ball thread make sm p and 1 ds (2nd center p made). Rw, ch of 10 ds. R of 4 ds, join to last p of previous r, 5 ds, 2 p's sep. by 5 ds, 4 ds, cl. Ch of 10 ds, join to 2nd center p; ch of 11 ds. R of 5 ds, join to last p of previous r, 6 ds, 2 p's sep.

by 6 ds, 5 ds, cl. Ch of 11 ds, join to 2nd center p.

On ball thread make sm p and 1 ds (3rd center p made). Rw, ch of 12 ds. R of 6 ds, join to last p of previous r, 7 ds, 2 p's sep. by 7 ds, 6 ds, cl. Ch of 12 ds, join to 3rd center p; ch of 13 ds. R of 7 ds, join to last p of previous r, 8 ds, 2 p's sep. by 8 ds, 7 ds, cl. Ch of 13 ds, join to 3rd center p; ch of 12 ds. R of 6 ds, join to last p of previous r, 7 ds, 2 p's sep. by 7 ds, 6 ds, cl. Ch of 12 ds, join to 3rd center p.

Rw, ch of 11 ds. R of 5 ds, join to last p of previous r, 6 ds, 2 p's sep. by 6 ds, 5 ds, cl. Ch of 11 ds, join to 2nd center p, ch of 10 ds. R of 4 ds, join to last p of previous r, 5 ds, 2 p's sep. by 5 ds, 4 ds, cl. Ch of 10 ds, join to

2nd center p; ch of 9 ds. R of 3 ds, join to last p of previous r, 4 ds, 2 p's sep. by 4 ds, 3 ds, cl. Ch of 9 ds, join to 1st center p; ch of 8 ds. R of 2 ds, join to last p of previous r, 3 ds, 2 p's sep. by 3 ds, 2 ds, cl. Ch of 8 ds, join to 1st center p. Tie and cut.

Make 10 more motifs same as this, joining the center p of first and second r's to the center p's of the corresponding r's of previous motif.

EDGING ... Use two shuttles. **1st row:** Tie threads to the free p of the 3rd r at free end of 1st motif. Holding r's toward you, make ch of 4 ds. R of 5 ds, join to free p of 4th r of motif, 5 ds, cl. * Ch of 12 ds, join to free p of next r; ch of 8 ds, p, 8 ds, join to free p of next (center) r of motif; ch of 8

Continued on page 46

Cameo Collar

Materials Required—AMERICAN THREAD COMPANY "STAR" MERCERIZED TATTING COTTON

3—75 Yd. Balls White or Color.

½ Yd. Dimity or any Dainty Material.

To make Collar. Cut 2 triangles measuring 6 inches at top edge, 8¼ inches at outer edge and 9 inches at inside edge.

Cut a strip of ruffling 65 inches long and 1¾ inch wide. Take one end of ruffling and sew around the 8¼ inch and 6 inch side of triangle, fulling it slightly at side and making it quite full at corner. Do the same with other end of ruffling on second triangle leaving the center section of ruffling for back of neck. Take 28 inches of bias tape and beginning at outer edge of ruffle bind the neck edge of ruffle and triangle. Do the same with second triangle, then bind the remainder of ruffling for back of neck, shirring the ruffle to fit. Make a very narrow hem on outer edge of ruffle.

Tatted Edging. One Shuttle only required.

R, 3 d, 5 p sep by 3 d, 3 d, cl r, turn, ⅛ inch space.

R, 3 d, long p, 3 d, s p, 6 d, cl r, turn. * ⅛ inch space. R, 3 d, join to last p of large r, 3 d, 4 p sep by 3 d, 3 d, cl r, turn. ⅛ inch space. R, 6 d, p, 6 d, cl r, turn. Repeat from *. ⅛ inch space. Work 3 large r joining same as other large rings, turn. ⅛ inch space. R, 6 d, join to p of last small r, 6 d, cl r, turn. ⅛ inch space. R, 3 d, join to p of large r, 3 d, 4 p, sep by 3 d, 3 d, cl r, turn. Work 2 large rings joining them same as other large rings, turn. ⅛ inch space. R, 6 d, join to 2 small r, 6 d, cl r, turn. ⅛ inch space. R, 3 d, join to large ring, 3 d, 4 p sep by 3 d, 3 d, cl r, turn. ⅛ inch space. R, 6 d, join to p of corresponding r, 6 d, cl r, turn. ⅛ inch space. R, 3 d, join to last p of last r, 3 d, 4 p sep by 3 d, 3 d, close r, turn. ⅛ inch space. R, 6 d, join the small p of opposite r, 3 d, long p, 3 d, cl r. ⅛ inch space. Work 1 more large r joining to large r, break thread.

Work a 2nd motif joining it to 1st motif at center p of 3 large rings. Work as many motifs as desired.

With a crochet needle join thread in 1st p of large r, ch 3, s c in p of small r, ch 3, s c in p of next small r, ch 3, s c in p of next large r, ch 3, repeat from beginning across straight edge of motifs.

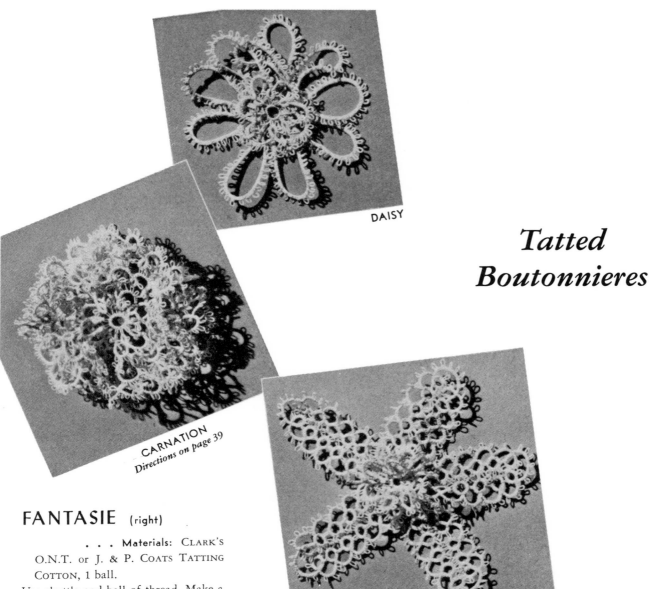

DAISY

CARNATION
Directions on page 39

Tatted Boutonnieres

FANTASIE (right)

. . . Materials: CLARK'S O.N.T. or J. & P. COATS TATTING COTTON, 1 ball.

Use shuttle and ball of thread. Make a center ring of 1 ds, 14 p's sep. by 1 ds, 1 ds, cl. Tie and cut.

1st rnd: R of 3 ds, p, 3 ds, join to p of center ring, 3 ds, p, 3 ds, cl. * Rw, ch of 4 ds, 5 p's sep. by 2 ds, 4 ds. Rw, r of 3 ds, p, 3 ds, join to next p of center ring, 3 ds, p, 3 ds, cl. Repeat from * around, joining last ch to base of first r of this rnd. Tie and cut.

POINT . . . R of 4 ds, p, 3 ds, 3 p's sep. by 2 ds, 3 ds. p, 4 ds, cl. * Rw, ch of 3 ds, 3 p's sep. by 3 ds, 3 ds. Rw, r of 4 ds, join to last p of previous r. 3 ds, 3 p's sep. by 2 ds, 3 ds, p, 4 ds, cl. Repeat from * 4 more times. Rw, ch of 3 ds, 6 p's sep. by 3 ds, 3 ds. Rw, r of 4 ds, p, 3 ds, p, 2 ds, join to center p of previous r, 2 ds, p, 3 ds, p, 4 ds, cl. ** Rw, ch of 3 ds, 3 p's sep. by 3 ds, 3 ds. Rw, r of 4 ds, join to last p of previous r, 3 ds, p, 2 ds, join to center p of opposite r, 2 ds, p, 3 ds, p, 4 ds, cl.

Repeat from ** 4 more times. Rw, ch of 4 ds. This completes one point.

Do not tie or cut but make 4 more points, joining first p of first ch on each point to last p of last ch on each point, and joining last ch of 4 ds to base of 1st r on first point. Tie and cut. With needle and thread, draw up p's at center of points and sew neatly to back of center ring.

DAISY (Top)

. . . Materials: CLARK'S O.N.T. or J. & P. COATS TATTING COTTON, 1 ball.

Use shuttle and ball of thread. Make a center ring of 1 ds, 20 p's sep. by 1 ds, 1 ds, cl. Tie and cut. **1st rnd:** R of 3 ds, p, 3 ds, join to p of center ring, 3 ds, p, 3 ds, cl. * Rw, ch of 4 ds, 5 p's sep. by 2 ds, 4 ds. Rw, r of 3 ds, p, 3 ds, skip one p on center ring, join to next p, 3 ds, p, 3 ds, cl. Repeat from * 8 more times (10 r's made). Rw, ch of 4 ds, 5 p's sep. by 2 ds, 4 ds, join at base of first r of 1st rnd. Tie and cut. **2nd rnd:** Join thread in a free p of center ring. * Ch of 6 ds, 26 p's sep. by 3 ds, 6 ds, join to next free p of center ring. Repeat from * around. Join last ch to p where thread was joined. Tie and cut.

Medallion Baby Cap

Materials: J. & P. Coats Tatting Cotton, 3 balls, size 70. 1 shuttle.

Center medallion: R, 1 d s, 1 lp (lp's are made only in center rings of medallions, others are regular p's). * 2 d s, 1 lp, repeat from * 8 more times, 1 d s, close and fasten off. R, 2 d s, join to 1st lp of r just made, 2 d s, close. Turn, leave ⅛ inch of thread clear, r, * 3 d s, p, repeat from * 4 more times, 3 d s, close. (This is an edge ring.) ** Turn, leave ⅛ inch of thread clear, r, 2 d s, join to next lp of center r, 2 d s, close. Turn, leave ⅛ inch of thread clear, r, 3 d s, join to next p of edge ring, * 3 d s, p, repeat from * 3 more times, 3 d s, close. Repeat from ** around, until 10 edge rings are made. Join and fasten off.

Medallion edging: R, 3 d s, p, 3 d s, join to center p of any ring of medallion, 3 d s, p, 3 d s, close. (This is an inner ring of edge.) Turn, leave ⅛ inch of thread clear, r, * 3 d s, p, and repeat from * 4 more times, 3 d s, close. (This is an outer ring of edge.) Turn. ** Leave ⅛ inch of thread clear, r, 3 d s, join to last p of inner ring previously made, 3 d s, join to same p of medallion to which 1st inner ring was joined, 3 d s,

p, 3 d s, close. Turn. Leave ⅛ inch of thread clear, r, 3 d s, join to last p of outer ring of edge. * 3 d s, p, and repeat from * 3 more time, 3 d s, close. Turn, leave ⅛ inch of thread clear, r, 3 d s, join to p of adjoining inner ring, 3 d s, join to center p of next ring of medallion, 3 d s, p, 3 d s, close. Turn. R, 3 d s, join to last p of adjoining outer ring, * 3 d s, p, and repeat from * 3 more times, 3 d s, close. Turn, and repeat from ** around medallion. Join and fasten off.

1st rnd of medallions around center one: Medallions for rest of cap are made the same as the center medallion without the edging, but for the 1st ring of medallions in the 1st rnd, make 8 lp's with 2 d s between, instead of 10 (making 8 edge rings). Join 1 edge ring of 1st medallion to center p of any ring of center medallion edging. Finish medallion and break off. There are 9 more medallions in 1st rnd, joined to center p of every other ring of center medallion edging, and joined together by center p's of 2 rings (adjacent to ring joining center medallion). This leaves 3 rings free on outer edge of this rnd.

2nd rnd of medallions: (12 medallions.) From

here on, medallions are made with 12 lp's in the 1st ring. 3 rings of each medallion are joined to the adjacent ones in the rnd. Leave 4 rings free on the outer edge, and join the 2 inner rings to the previous rnd—the 1st to 1 medallion and the 2nd to the adjacent one. This completes the circular motif of the back. The rest of the cap is made in rows.

1st row: (10 medallions). Work a medallion joining 4 adjacent rings to the last rnd—the 1st and 2nd rings to the last 2 free rings of one medallion, and the 3rd and 4th to the 1st 2 free rings of the next medallion, and join the medallions of the row together by the two rings adjacent to the joining to the previous rnd. (When the row is completed it leaves 3 medallions of the last rnd to form part of the bottom of the cap.)

2nd row: This row begins and ends with a small double clover leaf motif made as follows: R, * 3 d s, p, repeat from * 4 more time, 3 d s, close. Leave ⅛ inch of thread, r, 3 d s, join to last p of ring just made, 3 d s, p, 3 d s, join to center p of 3rd ring from joining of 1st 2 medallions of previous row, 3 d s, p, 3 d s, p, 3 d s, close. ** Leave ⅛ inch of thread clear, r, 3 d s, join to last p of preceding ring, * 3 d s, p, and repeat from * 3 more times, 3 d s, close **. Repeat between **'s 3 more times, joining the last ring to the 1st p of 1st ring of the motif. Break off and fasten by tying the ends through the loop between the 3rd and 4th rings of the motif. This row is made of 9 medallions and the 2 motifs. Work a medallion and attach 1 ring to the 1 top ring of the small motif, the adjacent 2 rings to the 2 free rings of the preceding row, and the next 2 rings to the 1st 2 free rings of the next medallion. The medallion in the row are joined together by 2 rings. (This leaves 4 rings free on the outer edge.)

3rd row: (10 medallions). The medallions in the row are joined together by 3 adjacent rings. Start the row by joining one ring to the end ring of the small motif, and the next 2 rings to the 1st 2 free rings of the 1st medallion of the preceding row. The next medallion joins to the 2 adjacent rings of this same medallion of the preceding row.

Finish across bottom of cap with a row of insertion as follows: R, 2 d s, 1 lp, 2 d s, join to center p of 4th free ring of 1st edge medallion, 2 d s, 1 l p, 2 d s, close. Turn, leave ⅛ inch of thread clear, r, 2 d s, 1 lp, 3 d s, p, 2 d s, close. Turn, leave ⅛ inch thread clear, r, 2 d s, join to last p of adjacent ring, 3 d s, 1 lp, 2 d s, close. Turn. Continue working insertion in this way, joining every other ring on inner edge to the 3 free rings of the edge of medallions, and making 2 rings between the medallions.

Carnation
Shown on page 37

. . . Materials: CLARK'S O.N.T. or J. & P. COATS TATTING COTTON, 1 ball.

Use shuttle and ball of thread. Make a center ring of 2 ds, 12 p's sep. by 2 ds, 2 ds, cl. Tie and cut. **1st rnd:** R of 3 ds, p, 3 ds, join to p of center ring, 3 ds, p, 3 ds, cl. * Rw, ch of 4 ds, 5 p's sep. by 2 ds, 4 ds. Rw, r of 3 ds, p, 3 ds, join to next p of center ring, 3 ds, p, 3 ds, cl. Repeat from * around, joining last ch to base of first r of 1st rnd. Tie and cut.

2nd and 3rd rnds: * R of 3 ds, p, 3 ds, join to first p of ch on previous rnd, 3 ds, p, 3 ds, cl. Rw, ch of 4 ds, 5 p's sep. by 2 ds, 4 ds. Rw, r of 3 ds, p, 3 ds, join to center p of same ch on previous rnd, 3 ds, p, 3 ds, cl. Rw, ch of 4 ds, 5 p's sep. by 2 ds, 4 ds. Rw, r of 3 ds, p, 3 ds, join to last p of same ch on previous rnd, 3 ds, p, 3 ds, cl. Rw, ch of 4 ds, 5 p's sep. by 2 ds, 4 ds. Repeat from * around, joining last ch to base of first r of 2nd rnd. Tie and cut.

Victory

MATERIALS:

CLARK'S O.N.T. or **J. & P. COATS BEST SIX CORD MERCERIZED CROCHET**, size 30, 1 ball.

Use shuttle and ball of thread.

FILL-IN MOTIFS (Make 2) . . .
R of 3 ds, 3 p's sep. by 3 ds, 3 ds, cl. Rw, ch of 8 ds, p, 4 ds, p, 4 ds. * Rw, r of 3 ds, 3 p's sep. by 3 ds, 3 ds, cl. Rw, ch of 4 ds, 3 p's sep. by 4 ds, 4 ds. Repeat from * 2 more times. Mark the last p made as p of turning ch to which outer edge of collar is joined later. Continue to work outside edge of fill-in motif as follows: Rw, r of 3 ds, p, 3 ds, join to center p of previous r, 3 ds, p, 3 ds, cl. ** Rw, ch of 4 ds, 3 p's sep. by 4 ds, 4 ds. Rw, r of 3 ds, p, 3 ds, join to center p of opposite r, 3 ds, 3 ds, cl. Repeat from ** once more. Rw, ch of 4 ds, 3 p's sep. by 4 ds, 4 ds. Rw, r of 3 ds, p, 3 ds, join to center p of 1st r made, 3 ds, p, 3 ds, cl. This completes one half of fill-in motif. Rw, ch of 4 ds, 3 p's sep. by 4 ds, 4 ds. Rw, for second half make r of 3 ds, p, 3 ds, join to same p as previous r, 3 ds, p, 3 ds, cl. Continue around making second half same as first. After last r make a ch of 4 ds, p, 4 ds, join to opposite p of 1st ch, 8 ds, join to base of 1st r. Tie and cut. Mark corresponding p of 2nd turning ch in same manner as on other side.

OUTER EDGE OF COLLAR . . .

R of 4 ds, 3 p's sep. by 4 ds, 4 ds, cl. (R of 4 ds, join to last p of previous r, 4 ds, p, 4 ds, p, 4 ds, cl) twice—*clover made.* * Rw, ch of 8 ds. Rw, r of 4 ds, p, 4 ds, join to center p of last r, 4 ds, p, 4 ds, cl. Finish clover. Repeat from * once more — *cluster made.* Rw, ch of 8 ds, p, 8 ds. Rw, sr of 3 ds, join to center p of last r, 3 ds, p, 3 ds, p, 3 ds, cl. Rw, ch of 8 ds, p, 8 ds. Rw, r of 4 ds, 3 p's sep. by 4 ds, 4 ds, cl. R of 4 ds, join to last p of previous r, 4 ds, join to 3rd p of sr, 4 ds, p, 4 ds, cl. R of 4 ds, join to p of previous r, 4 ds, p, 4 ds, p, 4 ds, cl. Finish cluster. Rw, ch of 8 ds, join to p of opposite ch, 8 ds, p, 8 ds. Rw, sr of 3 ds, join to center p of last r, 3 ds, p, 3 ds, p, 3 ds, cl. Rw, ch of 8 ds, join to marked p of fill-in motif, 8 ds, p, 8 ds. Rw, make another cluster as before. Rw, ch of 8 ds,

Continued on page 45

Romance

MATERIALS:

CLARK'S O.N.T. or J. & P. COATS BEST SIX CORD MERCERIZED CROCHET, size 30.

CLARK'S O.N.T.—2 balls of White, Ecru or any color,

OR

J. & P. COATS —1 ball of White, Ecru or any color.

Use shuttle and ball of thread.

Starting at neckline work neckband as follows: R of 4 ds, 3 p's sep. by 4 ds, 4 ds, cl. Rw, sp (¼ inch), r of 4 ds, 3 p's sep. by 4 ds, 4 ds, cl. * Rw, sp (¼ inch), r of 4 ds, join to corresponding p of adjacent r, 4 ds, p, 4 ds, p, 4 ds, cl. Repeat from * across until piece measures 15 inches (or desired length). Tie and cut.

TOP RUFFLE . . . 1st row: R of 4 ds, p, 4 ds, join to 2nd (center) p of 1st r of neckband, 4 ds, p, 4 ds, cl. * Rw, ch of 5 ds, p, 5 ds. Rw, r of 4 ds, p, 4 ds, join to free p of next r of neckband, 4 ds, p, 4 ds, cl. Repeat from * across ending with a ring. **2nd row:** * Ch of 3 ds, 5 p's sep. by 3 ds, 3 ds. Rw, r of 4 ds, p, 4 ds, join to p of adjacent ch, 4 ds, p, 4 ds, cl. Rw. Repeat from * across joining last ch to base of 1st r of 1st row. Tie and cut.

BOTTOM RUFFLE . . . 1st row: R of 4 ds, p, 4 ds, join to 2nd (center) p of 1st r of neckband, 4 ds, p, 4 ds, cl. * Rw, ch of 3 ds, p, 3 ds. Rw, r of 4 ds, p, 4 ds, join to free p of next r of neckband, 4 ds, p, 4 ds, cl. Repeat from * across ending with a ring. **2nd row:** Ch of 3 ds, p, 3 ds. * R of 4 ds, 3 p's sep. by 4 ds, 4 ds, cl. Rw, ch of 5 ds, join to p of adjacent ch, 5 ds. Rw. Repeat from * across ending with 1 r after last joining. **3rd row:** Rw, ch of 3 ds, 5 p's sep. by 3 ds, 3 ds. * Rw, r of 4 ds, p, 4 ds, join to center p of adjacent r, 4 ds, p, 4 ds, cl. Rw, ch of 3 ds, 3 p's sep. by 2 ds, 3 ds. Repeat from * across ending with ch of 3 ds, 5 p's sep. by 3 ds, 3 ds, join to base of 1st r of previous row. Tie and cut. **4th row:** R of 4 ds, p, 4 ds, join to center p of 3-p ch, 4 ds, p, 4 ds, cl. * Rw, ch of 3 ds, 4 p's sep. by 2 ds, 3 ds. Rw, r of 4 ds, p, 4 ds, join to center p of next ch, 4 ds, p, 4 ds, cl. Repeat from * ending with a ring. Tie and cut.

Spun Sugar
Accessories

Boutonnière Page 43

Collar Page 43

Wildflower Earrings

Daisy Earrings (left)

MATERIALS:

J. & P. COATS TATTING COTTON,
1 ball is sufficient for a few pairs
of earrings.

2 earring bases.

Sr of 3 ds, 3 sm p's sep. by 3 ds, 3 ds,
cl. Lr of 2 ds, sm p, * 2 ds, 8 lp's sep.
by 2 ds, 2 ds, sm p, 2 ds, cl. Sp ⅛ inch,
lr of 2 ds, join to sm p of preceding
lr. Repeat from * until 12 lr's are
made. Tie and cut.

Finishing . . . Gather into a cluster
and sew to first sr. Fasten piece to
earring base and stiffen the tatting by
brushing lightly with colorless nail
enamel. Finish other earring in same
way.

Wild Rose Earrings (right)

MATERIALS:

J. & P. COATS TATTING COTTON,
1 ball is sufficient for a few pairs
of earrings.

2 earring bases.

Sr of 3 ds, 3 sm p's sep. by 3 ds, 3 ds,
cl. * R of 8 ds, part cl (that is, leave
⅛-inch sp at base of r). Sp ⅛ inch.
Repeat from * until 4 r's are made.
Then continue with r's as before,
making 4 r's of 12 ds, 4 of 16 ds,
4 of 18 ds, 4 of 20 ds, and 5 of 22 ds,
always leaving ⅛ inch between r's.
Tie and cut.

Finishing . . . Gather into a cluster
and sew to first sr. Fasten piece to
earring base and stiffen the tatting by
brushing lightly with colorless nail
enamel. Finish other earring in same
way.

Boutonnière

MATERIALS:

J. & P. COATS TATTING COTTON,
1 ball.

1¼ yards contrasting color narrow
ribbon.

MOTIF . . . R of 4 ds, sm p, 3 ds,
7 p's sep. by 2 ds, 3 ds, sm p, 4 ds,
cl. R of 4 ds, join to sm p of preceding r, 3 ds, 7 p's sep. by 2 ds, 3 ds,
sm p, 4 ds, cl. Make 3 more r's like
2nd r, joining last r to 1st r at sm p.
Tie and cut.

The boutonnière is made of two
rounds of motifs.

Outer rnd . . . Make 18 motifs joining them to each other at the center p
of r's so that there are 2 r's free on
each motif along one edge (outer
edge) and 1 r free along other edge
(inner edge). Join last motif to 1st
one. Tie and cut.

Inner rnd . . . Make 9 motifs joining them together in the same way,
but joining each free r (2 on each
motif) to a free r on inner edge of
outer rnd.

For the center, cut a circle of linen,
1 inch in diameter, and make a narrow hem all around it. Sew the 9 free
r's to the outside of this linen center.
Starch lightly and finish with a ribbon
rosette.

Collar

MATERIALS:

J. & P. COATS TATTING COTTON,
2 balls.

¼ yard of organdie, 36 inches wide.

1 yard bias binding.

1st row: Starting at front edge, make
* r of 4 ds, p, 4 ds, cl. Rw, ch of
8 ds, p, 8 ds. Repeat from * until
19 ch's are made. To make corner of
collar, make r of 4 ds, p, 4 ds, cl. Rw,
ch of 8 ds, p, 8 ds. Rw, r of 4 ds,
join to p of preceding r, 4 ds, cl. Then
rw, and continue making r's and ch's
alternately as before until 46 ch's are
made for back. For the other corner,
make another group of 2 r's joined at
the p, with a ch between the r's. Make
19 more r's and ch's for the other
front, ending with an r. Tie and cut.
2nd row: R of 4 ds, p, 4 ds, cl. Rw,
ch of 9 ds, p, 9 ds. Rw, r of 4 ds,
join to p in 1st ch of 1st row, 4 ds,
cl. * Rw, ch of 9 ds, p, 9 ds. Rw,
r of 4 ds, join to p in next ch of
previous row. Repeat from * to end
of row, at each corner making 2 r's
joined to the p of corner ch in previous row and having end of row correspond with beginning. **3rd row:** Work
as for 2nd row, but making ch's of
10 ds, p, 10 ds. **4th row:** Work as for
previous row, but making ch's of 9 ds,
3 p's sep. by 2 ds, 9 ds.

Cut 2 rectangular pieces of organdie
each 5½ x 8 inches. Cut each piece
diagonally across, thus having 4 triangles each 5½ x 8 x 9¾ inches.
Place 2 pieces together and machine
stitch along the two shorter sides of
triangle. Turn right side out. Make
other lapel in same way, then finish
the remaining side of each lapel with
bias binding, leaving 6 inches of binding between the 2 lapels for back of
neck and 1 inch of binding free at
front ends of collar. Sew tatting to
collar through the p's of the small r's
on the 1st row, easing in lace to form
frill. Fasten the ends of each row of
tatting to the 1-inch pieces of binding
left at the front ends of collar.

Heirlooms
for Your Baby

BABY BONNET

Materials Required: AMERICAN THREAD COMPANY "STAR" MERCERIZED CROCHET COTTON, Article 30

Size 50

2—175 yd. Balls White.
2 yds. Narrow Ribbon.
1 yd. 1 inch Ribbon.
1 Shuttle and 1 Ball.

Motif. R, 3 d, 3 p sep by 3 d, 3 d, cl r. R, 4 d, join to last p of previous r, 7 d, p, 7 d, p, 4 d, cl r. R, 3 d, join to last p of previous r, 3 d, 2 p sep by 3 d, 3 d, cl r, (clover) * turn. Ch, 8 d, p, 8 d, 3 p sep by 4 d, 8 d, p, 8 d, turn. R, 3 d, p, 3 d, join to corresponding p of small r, 3 d, p, 3 d, cl r. R, 4 d, join to last p of previous r, 7 d, join to center p of large r, 7 d, p, 4 d, cl r. R, 3 d, join to last p of previous r, 3 d, 2 p sep by 3 d, 3 d, cl r. Repeat from * twice joining last r to 1st r in corresponding p, turn. Ch, 8 d, p, 8 d, 3 p sep by 4 d, 8 d, p, 8 d, join, tie and cut.

Work a 2nd motif in same manner joining to 1st motif in following manner: Work a clover, turn. Ch, 8 d, p, 8 d, 2 p sep by 4 d, 4 d, join to corresponding p of 1st motif, 8 d, join to corresponding p of 1st motif, 8 d, turn. Work a clover, turn. Ch, 8 d, join to corresponding p of 1st motif, 8 d, join to corresponding p of 1st motif, 4 d, 2 p sep by 4 d, 8 d, p, 8 d and complete motif same as 1st motif.

Join 3rd motif to 1st motif, join 4th motif to 3rd and 2nd motifs. Continue until there are 12 x 5 motifs for front of cap. For back of cap, omit 4 motifs on each side and work 4 rows of 4 motifs.

Block and press. To make cap. Sew ribbon in position at top of cap and lace ribbon through motifs of side and back of cap to lower edge, sew in position. Finish other side in same manner. Sew ribbon to 1st motif at lower edge of cap and lace it to center back of cap. Cut ribbon leaving an end for tying. Sew another length of ribbon to 1st motif at lower edge on opposite side and lace to center back, cut and tie in bow. Attach ribbon ties as illustrated.

EDGING FOR DRESS

Materials Required: AMERICAN THREAD COMPANY "STAR" MERCERIZED TATTING COTTON Article 25

2—75 Yd. Balls White.
1 Shuttle and 1 Ball.

R, 4 d, 3 p sep by 3 d, 4 d, cl r. R, 4 d, 3 p sep by 3 d, 4 d, cl r, turn. * Ch, 5 d, 5 p sep by 2 d, 5 d, turn. R, 4 d, p, 3 d, join to center p of last r, 3 d, p, 4 d, cl r. R, 4 d, 3 p sep by 3 d, 4 d, cl r, turn. Repeat from * for length desired for lower edge of dress, neck and sleeves. The edging is sewed with the ring edge to material.

Petal Point Collar and Cuff Set
Continued from page 29

of 4 ds, p, 4 ds, join to center p of 1st r on 4th row, 4 ds, p, 4 ds, cl. * Rw, ch of 8 ds, p, 8 ds. Rw, r of 4 ds, p, 4 ds, skip 1 r, join to center p of next r, 4 ds, p, 4 ds, cl. Repeat from * until 57 r's and 56 ch's are made. Rw, ch of 8 ds, p, 8 ds. **6th row:** R of 6 ds, p, 6 ds, p, 6 ds, cl. * Rw, ch of 8 ds, join to p of ch on previous row, 8 ds, p, 8 ds. Rw, r of 6 ds, join to p of previous r, 6 ds, p, 6 ds, cl. Rw, ch of 8 ds, rw. R of 6 ds, join to previous p, 6 ds, p, 6 ds, cl. R of 6 ds, join to p of last r, 6 ds, p, 6 ds, cl. R of 6 ds, join to p of last r, 6 ds, p, 6 ds, cl. Rw, ch of 8 ds. Rw, r of 6 ds, join to p of previous r, 6 ds, p, 6 ds, cl. Rw, ch of 8 ds, join to p of adjacent ch, 8 ds, join to p of next ch on previous row, 8 ds, rw. R of 6 ds, join to p of previous r, 6 ds, p, 6 ds, cl. Repeat from * until 28 points are made. Rw, ch of 8 ds, p, 8 ds, join to base of last r on 5th row.

CUFFS . . . Work as for 4th, 5th and 6th rows of collar for desired length.

V-Neck Collar
Continued from page 33

Rw, ch of 6 ds, p, 6 ds. Rw, r of 5 ds, p, 4 ds, join to p of 10th ch of 1st row, 4 ds, p, 5 ds, cl. Rw, ch of 8 ds. Rw, r of 5 ds, join to center p of 11th ch, 4 ds, p, 4 ds, p, 5 ds, cl. Rw, ch of 8 ds. Rw, r of 5 ds, 3 p's sep. by 4 ds, 5 ds, cl. Join with a ds to the base of the opposite r. Rw, ch of 6 ds, join to p of opposite ch, 6 ds. ** Rw, r of 5 ds, 3 p's sep. by 4 ds, 5 ds, cl. Rw, ch of 8 ds, join to p of opposite ch, 8 ds. Repeat from ** 7 more times, joining last ch to base of 1st r made. Tie and cut. Make another strip at other end of collar.

2nd row: R of 5 ds, p, 4 ds, join to center p of 3-p chain of fill-in strip, 4 ds, p, 5 ds, cl. * Rw, ch of 8 ds, p, 8 ds. Rw, r of 5 ds, p, 4 ds, join to center p of next r of fill-in strip, 4 ds, p, 5 ds, cl. Repeat from * 8 more times. Rw, ch of 8 ds, p, 8 ds. Rw, r of 5 ds, p, 4 ds, join to adjacent p of next r, 4 ds, p, 5 ds, cl. Rw, ch of 8 ds, p, 8 ds. Rw, r of 5 ds, p, 4 ds, join to p of next ch of 1st row, 4 ds, p, 5 ds, cl. Continue to work across in this manner, joining the last r to center p of ch at end of collar. Do not cut threads, but make a ch of 8 ds, p, 8 ds, and turn.
EDGING . . . R of 5 ds, 3 p's sep. by 4 ds, 5 ds, cl. R of 5 ds, 3 p's sep. by 4 ds, 5 ds, cl. Rw, ch of 8 ds, join to p of 1st ch of previous row, 8 ds. * Rw, r of 7 ds, lp, 7 ds, cl. Rw, ch of 4 ds, p, 4 ds, join to center p of adjacent r, 4 ds, p, 4 ds. Rw, r of 7 ds, join to lp, 7 ds, cl. Rw, ch of 4 ds, 6 p's sep. by 2 ds, 4 ds. Rw, r of 7 ds, join to lp, 7 ds, cl. Rw, ch of 4 ds, 3 p's sep. by 4 ds, 4 ds. Rw, r of 7 ds, join to lp, 7 ds, cl.

Rw, ch of 8 ds, join to p of next ch of previous row, 8 ds. Rw, r of 5 ds, p, 4 ds, join to center p of adjacent ch, 4 ds, p, 5 ds, cl. R of 5 ds, 3 p's sep. by 4 ds, 5 ds, cl. Rw, ch of 8 ds, join to p of next ch of previous row, 8 ds. Repeat from * across collar, ending with a group of 2 r's. Do not reverse work, but make a ch of 8 ds, p, 8 ds, join at base of end r of 2nd row. Tie and cut.

Pleasure Bent
Continued from page 34

end of collar until the 6th r of the end motif is completed. Do not cut threads, but work inside edge of collar as follows: Rw, ch of 3 ds, p, 3 ds. Rw, make a 3-r group as follows: R of 2 ds, p, 2 ds, join to center p of adjacent ch, 2 ds, 3 p's sep by 2 ds, 2 ds, cl. Rw, ch of 3 ds, 3 p's sep by 3 ds, 3 ds. Rw, r of 2 ds, p, 2 ds, join to corresponding p of previous r, 2 ds, 3 p's sep by 2 ds, 2 ds, cl. Rw, ch of 3 ds, 3 p's sep by 3 ds, 3 ds. Rw, r of 2 ds, p, 2 ds, join to corresponding p of previous r, 2 ds, p, 2 ds, join to center p of next ch, 2 ds, p, 2 ds, cl (3-r group completed). Rw, ch of 4 ds, 3 p's sep by 4 ds, 4 ds. Rw, r of

2 ds, p, 2 ds, skip one p of turning chain of Fill-in Motif, join to next p of same turning chain, 2 ds, 3 p's sep by 2 ds, 2 ds, cl.
Finish this 3-r group, joining last r to center p of next ch of Fill-in Motif. Rw, ch of 4 ds, 3 p's sep by 4 ds, 4 ds. Rw, r of 2 ds, p, 2 ds, join to center p of next ch, 2 ds, 3 p's sep by 2 ds, 2 ds, cl. Finish this 3-r group, joining last r to center p of next ch of Fill-in Motif. Rw, ch of 4 ds, 3 p's sep by 4 ds, 4 ds. Rw, make another 3-r group, joining last r to first free p of turning chain of Fill-in Motif. Rw, ch of 4 ds, 3 p's sep by 4 ds, 4 ds. Rw, make a 3-r group, joining first r to center p of next 3-p ch, and joining last r to center p of following 3-p ch.
Make another ch and 3-r group same

as last ch and group. Rw, ch of 3 ds, 3 p's sep by 3 ds, 3 ds (a short chain). Continue across, alternating 3-r groups and short chains (joining as before) until there are 8 short chains. Finish remaining inside edge of collar to correspond. Join last ch to base of first r of outer edge of collar. Tie and cut.

CUFF (Make 2) . . . Make a Fill-in Motif. Then work as for outer edge of collar until seven 7-r motifs are completed. Work another single r. Do not reverse work, but make ch of 4 ds, 3 p's sep by 4 ds, 4 ds. Rw, start a 3-r motif as follows: R of 2 ds, p, 2 ds, join to center p of adjacent ch, 2 ds, 3 p's sep by 2 ds, 2 ds, cl. Finish 3-r motif and complete cuff as for ends of collar.

Victory
Continued from page 40

join to p of opposite ch, 8 ds, join to center p of next ch on fill-in motif, 8 ds. Rw, make a sr as before. Rw, ch of 8 ds, join to center p of next ch on fill-in motif, 8 ds, p, 8 ds. Rw, make a cluster as before. Rw, make a ch as before. Rw, make a sr as before. Rw, ch of 8 ds, join to 1st p of next ch on fill-in motif, finish ch, rw and make another cluster. Rw, ch of 8 ds, join to p of opposite ch, 8 ds, join last p of same ch of fill-in motif, 8 ds.
Work down other side of fill-in motif,

reversing work and joining to correspond with other side, making sr, ch, cluster, ch, sr, ch, cluster, ch of 8 ds, join to p on opposite ch, 8 ds, join to 1st p on end of fill-in motif, 8 ds. * Rw, sr. Rw, ch of 8 ds, p, 8 ds, p, 8 ds. Rw, cluster. Rw, ch of 8 ds, join to p on opposite ch, 8 ds, p, 8 ds. Repeat from * 9 more times. Rw, sr. Rw. Ch of 8 ds, join to marked p on 2nd fill-in motif, 8 ds, p, 8 ds. Continue around outer edge of fill-in motif (5 clusters). Rw, ch of 8 ds, join p on opposite ch, 8 ds, join to 1st p on end of fill-in motif, 8 ds. Rw, sr. Rw, ch of 8 ds, p, 8 ds, p, 8 ds. Rw, cluster. Rw, ch. Rw, sr. Rw, ch of 8 ds, p, 8 ds. Rw, cluster. * Rw, ch of 8 ds,

join to p of opposite ch, 8 ds. Rw, r of 4 ds, p, 4 ds, join to center p of previous r, 4 ds, p, 4 ds, cl. (R of 4 ds, join to last p of previous r, 4 ds, p, 4 ds, p, 4 ds, cl) twice (clover). Repeat from * 2 more times. Rw, ch of 8 ds, join to last p on end ch of fill-in motif, 8 ds. (Rw, make a clover. Rw, ch of 8 ds, join to center p of next ch on fill-in lace, 8 ds) twice. (Rw, clover. Rw, ch of 8 ds, join to center p on next full ch on fill-in lace, 8 ds) twice. Rw, clover. Rw, ch of 8 ds, join to last p on end ch of fill-in lace, 8 ds. * Rw, clover. Rw, ch of 8 ds, join to p of opposite ch, 8 ds. Repeat from * across having both ends correspond and tying last ch to base of 1st r made. Cut.

Necklace Collar
Continued from page 35

ds, p, 8 ds, join to free p of next r, ch of 12 ds.

With 2nd shuttle make a clover as follows: R of 5 ds, join to free p of next r, 5 ds, cl. R of 5 ds, join to free p of next r, 4 ds, join to first free p of next motif, 5 ds, cl. R of 5 ds, join to free p of next r, 5 ds, cl (clover made).

Working with 1st shuttle, repeat from * 9 more times. Ch of 12 ds, join to free p of next r, ch of 8 ds, p, 8 ds, join to free p of next (center) r, ch of 8 ds, p, 8 ds, join to free p of next r, ch of 12 ds. ** With 2nd shuttle, make r of 5 ds, join to free p of next r, 5 ds, cl. Repeat from ** once more. **2nd row:** Ch of 14 ds, p, 14 ds, join to thread at base of last 2 r's; ch of 12 ds, join to same p where p-ch of 1st row was joined, 8 ds, join to p of p-ch of 1st row.

*** Make a 3-leaf clover as follows: R of 4 ds, p, 5 ds, join to p of adjacent ch, 5 ds, p, 4 ds, cl; join to p at base of r. * R of 4 ds, join to adjacent p of last r, 5 ds, p, 4 ds, p, 4 ds, cl; join to p at base of r. Repeat from * once more (3-leaf clover made). Ch of 8 ds, join to center p of center r of motif, ch of 8 ds.

With 2nd shuttle make a 4-leaf clover as follows: R of 4 ds, p, 5 ds, skip 1 p of last r, join to next p, 5 ds, p, 4 ds, cl. ** R of 4 ds, join to adjacent p of last r, 5 ds, p, 5 ds, p, 4 ds, cl. Repeat from ** 2 more times (4-leaf clover made). With 1st shuttle make ch of 8 ds, join to same p where opposite ch was joined, ch of 8 ds, make a 3-leaf clover as before. Ch of 8 ds, join to p of next r of motif, 12 ds, join to thread at base of clover of 1st row, ch of 14 ds, skip 1 p of last r, join to next p, 14 ds, join to same thread at base of clover of 1st row, ch of 14 ds, p, 14 ds, join to same

thread at base of clover, ch of 12 ds, join to center p of r of motif to which next p-ch of 1st row was joined, 8 ds, join to p of p-ch of 1st row.

Repeat from *** until 11th group of 3 clovers is made. Ch of 8 ds, join to center p of next r of motif, 12 ds, join to base of 1st r of edging, ch of 14 ds, skip 1 p of last r, join to next p, 14 ds, join to base of 1st r of edging; ch of 5 ds, join to center p of 3rd r of 1st motif. Tie and cut.

HEADING . . . Tie threads to top p of 1st r of 1st motif. * Ch of 6 ds, p, 6 ds, join to 1st center p of same motif, ch of 6 ds, p, 6 ds, join to free p of next r, ch of 2 ds, p, 2 ds, join to free p of next r. Repeat from * across, joining last ch to top p of 1st r of last motif. Tie and cut.

With needle, run thread through p's of heading, adjusting to fit neckline. Tie at both ends. Cut thread.

Portrait
Continued from page 27

Outer Edge of Collar . . . R of 2 ds, 5 p's sep. by 2 ds, 2 ds, cl. * Rw, ch of 3 ds, 3 p's sep. by 3 ds, 3 ds. Rw, r of 2 ds, p, 2 ds, skip 1 p of previous r, join to next p, 2 ds, 3 p's sep. by 2 ds, 2 ds, cl. Repeat from * once more. Rw, ch of 3 ds, 3 p's sep. by 3 ds, 3 ds. R of 2 ds, 5 p's sep. by 2 ds, 2 ds, cl. Ch of 3 ds, 3 p's sep. by 3 ds, 3 ds. Rw, r of 2 ds, p, 2 ds, join to corresponding p of opposite r, 2 ds, 3 p's sep. by 2 ds, 2 ds, cl. Rw, ch of 3 ds, 3 p's sep. by 3 ds, 3 ds. Rw, r of 2 ds, p, 2 ds, join to corresponding p of last r, 2 ds, 3 p's sep. by 2 ds, 2 ds, cl. Rw, ch of 3 ds, 3 p's sep. by 3 ds, 3 ds. Rw, r of 2 ds, p, 2 ds, join to corresponding p of previous r, 2 ds, p, 2 ds, join to corresponding p of 1st r, 2 ds, p, 2 ds, cl (end motif, or point of collar completed).

Ch of 4 ds, 3 p's sep. by 4 ds, 4 ds. Work next motif as follows: R of 2 ds, 5 p's sep. by 2 ds, 2 ds, cl. Rw, ch of 3 ds, p, 3 ds, join to last p of adjacent ch of end motif, 3 ds, p, 3 ds. ** Rw, r of 2 ds, p, 2 ds, join to corresponding p of previous r, 2 ds, 3 p's sep. by 2 ds, 2 ds, cl. Rw, ch of 3 ds, p, 3 ds, 3 ds. Repeat from ** 4 more times.

Rw, r of 2 ds, p, 2 ds, join to corresponding p of previous r, 2 ds, p, 2 ds, join to corresponding p of 1st r of same motif, 2 ds, p, 2 ds, cl (7-ring motif completed). Ch of 3 ds, 3 p's sep. by 4 ds, 4 ds. Rw, make a single r of 2 ds, p, 2 ds, join to center p of last ch of

previous motif, 2 ds, 3 p's sep. by 2 ds, 2 ds, cl. Rw, make adjoining ch of 4 ds, p, 4 ds, join a marked p of turning ch of one fill-in motif, 4 ds, p, 4 ds.

Start next 7-ring motif as follows: R of 2 ds, 5 p's sep. by 2 ds, 2 ds, cl. Rw, ch of 3 ds, p, 3 ds, skip one p of single r, join to next p, 3 ds, p, 3 ds. Continue as for last motif until 7th r is completed. *** Make a joining ch of 4 ds, p, 4 ds, join to center p of next ch of outside edge of fill-in motif, 4 ds, p, 4 ds. Rw, make single r, joining to previous motif as before. Rw, make a joining ch of 4 ds, p, 4 ds, join to center p of next ch of fill-in motif, 4 ds, p, 4 ds. Make a 7-ring motif, joining 1st ch to last single r as before. Repeat from *** once more. Ch of 4 ds, p, 4 ds, join to same p of fill-in motif where last joining ch was joined, 4 ds, p, 4 ds. Rw.

Work and join as before the following: a single r, rw, a joining ch, a 7-ring motif, a joining ch, rw, a single r, rw, a joining ch, and a 7-ring motif. Continue as follows: Ch of 4 ds, p, 4 ds, join to other marked p of fill-in motif, 4 ds, p, 4 ds. **** Rw, make a single r, rw, ch of 4 ds, 3 p's sep. by 4 ds, 4 ds. Make a 7-ring motif, ch of 4 ds, 3 p's sep. by 4 ds, 4 ds. Repeat from **** 10 more times. Rw, make a single r. Ch of 4 ds, p, 4 ds, join to marked p of 2nd fill-in motif, 4 ds, p, 4 ds. Continue to work as for other end of collar until the 6th r of the end motif is completed. Do not cut threads, but work inside edge of collar as follows:

Rw, ch of 3 ds, p, 3 ds. Rw, make a 3-ring group as follows: R of 2 ds, p, 2 ds, join to center p of adjacent ch, 2 ds, 3 p's sep. by 2 ds, 2 ds, cl. Rw, ch of 3 ds, p, 3 ds, 3 ds. Rw, r of 2 ds, p, 2 ds, join to corresponding p of previous r, 2 ds, p, 2 ds, 2 ds,

cl. Rw, ch of 3 ds, 3 p's sep. by 3 ds, 3 ds. r of 2 ds, p, 2 ds, join to corresponding p of previous r, 2 ds, p, 2 ds, join to center p of next ch, 2 ds, p, 2 ds, cl (3-ring group completed). Rw, ch of 4 ds, 3 p's sep. by 4 ds, 4 ds. Rw, r of 2 ds, p, 2 ds, skip one p of turning ch of fill-in motif, join to next p of same turning ch, 2 ds, 3 p's sep. by 2 ds, 2 ds, cl.

Finish this 3-ring group, joining last r to center p of next ch of fill-in motif. Rw, ch of 4 ds, 3 p's sep. by 4 ds, 4 ds. Rw, r of 2 ds, p, 2 ds, join to center p of next ch, 2 ds, 3 p's sep. by 2 ds, 2 ds, cl. Finish this 3-ring group, joining last r to center p of next ch of fill-in motif. Rw, ch of 4 ds, 3 p's sep. by 4 ds, 4 ds. Rw, make another 3-ring group, joining last r to 1st free p of turning ch of fill-in motif. Rw, ch of 4 ds, 3 p's sep. by 4 ds, 4 ds. Rw, make a 3-ring group, joining 1st r to center p of next 3-p chain, and joining last r to center p of following 3-p chain.

Make another ch and 3-ring group same as last ch and group. Rw, ch of 3 ds, 3 p's sep. by 3 ds, 3 ds (a short ch). Continue across, alternating 3-ring groups and short chains (joining as before) until there are 8 short ch's. Finish remaining inside edge of collar to correspond. Join last ch to base of 1st r of outer edge of collar. Tie and cut.

CUFFS . . . Make a fill-in motif. Then work as for outer edge of collar until seven 7-ring motifs are completed. Work another single r. Do not reverse work, but make ch of 4 ds, 3 p's sep. by 4 ds, 4 ds. Rw, start a 3-ring motif as follows: R of 2 ds, p, 2 ds, join to center p of adjacent ch, 2 ds, 3 p's sep. by 2 ds, 2 ds, cl. Finish 3-ring motif, and complete cuff as for ends of collar. Make another same as this.

LUNCHEON SETS, PLACEMATS AND OTHER TABLE LINENS

"Cutwork" Luncheon Set

Materials: CLARK'S O.N.T. BEST SIX CORD MERCERIZED CROCHET, size 20, 5 balls of White or Ecru.

OR

J. & P. COATS BEST SIX CORD MERCERIZED CROCHET, size 20, 3 balls of White or Ecru.

3⅛ yds. of linen, 36 inches wide.

These materials are sufficient for a luncheon set consisting of a center mat 15 x 33 inches, 6 place mats 11 x 16½ inches, and 6 napkins, each about 16½ inches square.

PLACE MATS (Make 6) . . . Cut 6 pieces of linen, each 12½ x 18 inches. Make a ½-inch hem all around, with hem-stitching.

Corner Motif (Make 4 for each mat) . . . Use shuttle and ball of thread.

Flower . . . 1st rnd: With shuttle make r of 2 ds, 4 p's sep. by 3 ds, 1 ds. cl. Tie ends securely and cut. 2nd rnd: Tie shuttle and ball threads to one p of r. * Make a ch of 2 ds, p, 2 ds, p, 2 ds, join to next p of r. Repeat from * around. Tie ends and cut. 3rd rnd: Tie threads to one p of previous rnd.

* Make a ch of 3 ds, p, 3 ds, join to next p. Repeat from * around. Tie ends securely and cut off ball thread (8 scallops in rnd).

Spray . . . With shuttle, sp (¼-inch). R of 4 ds, join to adjacent p of 3rd rnd, 8 ds, p, 4 ds, p, 8 ds, cl. Rw. Leave no sp. R of 4 ds, join to adjacent p of 3rd rnd, 8 ds, p, 4 ds, p, 8 ds, cl. Insert tip of shuttle in the space to the right of the ¼-inch thread, and fasten securely (as for joining to a p). One group of 2 rings is made.

Continued on page 67

Grapevine Luncheon Set

SERVICE FOR FOUR

. . . **Materials:** CLARK'S O.N.T. BEST SIX CORD MERCERIZED CROCHET, size 30, 3 balls of White or Ecru, or 4 balls of any color.

OR

J. & P. COATS BEST SIX CORD MERCERIZED CROCHET, size 30, 3 balls of White, Ecru or any color.

1⅛ yds. of linen, 36 inches wide.

Above material is sufficient for a luncheon set consisting of a center mat about 14 x 36 inches, and 4 place mats about 12 x 18 inches. Edging measures about 1¾ inches wide.

CENTER MAT . . . Cut linen 14½ x 32½ inches. Make a narrow hem all around. Use shuttle and ball of thread.

1st row: Make r of 4 ds, p, 3 ds, 3 p's sep. by 2 ds, 3 ds, p, 4 ds, cl. Rw, make another r like this. Rw, ch of 9 ds. Rw, make a clover as follows: R of 4 ds, join to last p of adjacent r, 3 ds, 3 p's sep. by 2 ds, 3 ds, p, 4 ds, cl. Lr of 4 ds, join to last p of last r, 3 ds, 5 p's sep. by 2 ds, 3 ds, p, 4 ds, cl. R of 4 ds, join to last p of last lr, 3 ds, 3 p's sep. by 2 ds, 3 ds, p, 4 ds, cl (the last 3 r's form clover).

* Rw, ch of 9 ds. R of 4 ds, p, 3 ds, p, 2 ds, join to center p of adjacent r, 2 ds, p, 3 ds, p, 4 ds, cl. Rw, r of 4 ds, join to last p of adjacent r, 3 ds, 3 p's sep. by 2 ds, 3 ds, p, 4 ds, cl. Ch of 5 ds. Rw, r of 4 ds, join to last p of adjacent r, 3 ds, 3 p's sep. by 2 ds, 3 ds, p, 4 ds, cl. Rw, r of 4 ds, join to last p of adjacent r, 3 ds, 3 p's sep. by 2 ds, 3 ds, p, 4 ds, cl. Ch of 9 ds. Rw, make a clover as before. Rw, ch of 9 ds. R of 4 ds, p, 3 ds, p, 2 ds, join to center p of adjacent r, 2 ds, p, 3 ds, p, 4 ds, cl. Rw, r of 4 ds, join to last p of adjacent r, 3 ds, 3 p's sep. by 2 ds, 3 ds, p, 4 ds, cl. Rw, r of 4 ds, join to last p of adjacent r, 3 ds, 3 p's sep. by 2 ds, 3 ds, p, 4 ds, cl. Ch of 5 ds. Rw, r of 4 ds, join to last p of adjacent r, 3 ds, 3 p's sep. by 2 ds, 3 ds, p, 4 ds, cl. Rw, r of 4

ds, join to last p of adjacent r, 3 ds, 3 p's sep. by 2 ds, 3 ds, p, 4 ds, cl. Rw, ch of 9 ds. Rw, make a clover. Repeat from * until piece measures the length of one short side of center mat. Tie ends and cut.

Tie threads to 2nd p of lr of clover. **2nd row:** * Ch of 3 ds, p, 3 ds, skip 1 p, join to next p, ch of 3 ds, 6 p's sep. by 3 ds, 3 ds, rw. R of 5 ds, p, 5 ds, join to center p of next r of clover, 5 ds, p, 5 ds, cl. Rw, ch of 4 ds. Rw, r of 6 ds, p, 5 ds, join in same place where 2 r's of 1st row are joined (below clover), 5 ds, p, 6 ds, cl. Rw, ch of 4 ds. Rw, r of 5 ds, p, 5 ds, join to center p of first r of next clover, 5 ds, p, 5 ds, cl. Rw, ch of 3 ds, join to last p of adjacent ch, ch of 3 ds, 5 p's sep. by 3 ds, 3 ds, skip 1 p of lr of same clover, join to next p. Repeat from * across. Tie ends and cut. Sew to short side of center mat. Finish other side in same way.

PLACE MATS (Make 4) . . . Cut 4 pieces of material, each 12½ x 15 inches, and complete as for center mat.

Ariel

. . . **Materials:** CLARK'S O.N.T. BEST SIX CORD MERCERIZED CROCHET, size 20, 10 balls of White or Ecru.

OR

J. & P. COATS BEST SIX CORD MERCERIZED CROCHET, size 20, 8 balls of White or Ecru.

This material is sufficient for a luncheon set consisting of 4 place doilies about 11½ inches in diameter (from point to point), 4 bread and butter plate doilies about 8 inches in diameter, and 4 glass doilies about 5 inches in diameter.

PLACE DOILY . . . Use shuttle and ball of thread. **1st rnd:** Make a center-ring of 3 ds, 3 p's sep. by 3 ds, 3 ds, cl. Ch of 8 ds, p, 8 ds. Rw, r of 3 ds, 3 p's sep. by 3 ds, cl. Rw, ch of 8 ds, p, 8 ds. * Make a motif as follows: R of 6 ds, lp, 6 ds, cl. Rw, ch of 4 ds, 3 p's sep. by 4 ds, 4 ds. Rw, r of 6 ds, join to lp of previous r, 6 ds, cl. Rw, ch of 4 ds, 6 p's sep. by 2 ds, 4 ds. Rw, r of 6 ds, join to same lp, 6 ds, cl. Rw, ch of 4 ds, 3 p's sep. by 4 ds, 4 ds. Rw, r of 6 ds, join to same lp, 6 ds, cl (motif is now completed). Ch of 8 ds, join to p on opposite ch, 8 ds. Rw, r of 3 ds, 3 p's sep. by 3 ds, 3 ds, cl. Rw, ch of 8 ds, join to p on opposite ch, 8 ds (first point made).

Make center-ring of 3 ds, join to adjacent p of previous center ring, 3 ds, p, 3 ds, p, 3 ds, cl. Ch of 8 ds, p, 8 ds. Rw. r of 3 ds, p, 3 ds, join to center p of adjacent r, 3 ds, p, 3 ds, cl. Rw, ch of 8 ds, p, 8 ds. Repeat from * around, joining 8th center-ring to 1st p of 1st center ring made. Continue to work 8th point, joining last r to center p of adjacent r of 1st point. Join last ch to base of 1st ring made. Tie and cut.

Continued on page 53

Checkerboard

MATERIALS:

CLARK'S O.N.T. or J. & P. COATS BEST SIX CORD MERCERIZED CROCHET, size 20.

SMALL BALL:

CLARK'S O.N.T.—10 balls of White or Ecru,

OR

J. & P. COATS —6 balls of White or Ecru.

BIG BALL:

J. & P. COATS —3 balls of White or Ecru.

1 yard of linen, 18 inches wide.

This material is sufficient for a luncheon set consisting of a center mat about 16 inches square, 4 place mats about 11 inches square and 8 mats about 5½ inches square (4 for bread and butter plates and 4 for glasses).

CENTER MAT—First Corner . . . Use shuttle and ball of thread. **First Motif:** R of 6 ds, 3 p's sep. by 2 ds, 4 ds, cl. R of 4 ds, join to adjacent p of previous r, 2 ds, 4 p's sep. by 2 ds, 4 ds, cl. R of 4 ds, join to adjacent p of previous r, 2 ds, p, 2 ds, p, 6 ds, cl (clover leaf made). Rw, ch of 4 ds, p, 4 ds. * Rw, r of 6 ds, join to adjacent p of previous r, 2 ds, p, 2 ds, p, 4 ds, cl. Complete clover leaf as before. Rw, ch of 4 ds, join to p of previous ch, 4 ds. Repeat from * 2 more times, joining last r to adjacent p of 1st r made, and joining last ch to base of 1st r.

Second Motif . . . R of 6 ds, 3 p's sep. by 2 ds, 4 ds, cl. R of 4 ds, join to adjacent p of previous r, 2 ds, p, 2 ds, join to center p of corner of 1st motif, 2 ds, p, 2 ds, p, 4 ds, cl. R of 4 ds, join to adjacent p of previous r, 2 ds, p, 2 ds, p, 6 ds, cl. Rw and complete 2nd motif same as 1st motif.

Make 19 more motifs joining them as 2nd motif was joined to 1st (see illustration).

Work remaining 3 corners in same way, joining the corner p's of end motifs of outer edge to form a square. Cut an 11-inch square of linen. Place lace on linen; with a ruler and pencil draw a line lightly along inner edge of lace, having the lines touch the p's. Cut linen to within ¼ inch of line and make a narrow hem all around, having pencil mark at fold of hem. Sew lace to linen.

PLACE MATS (Make 4) . . . Make 10 motifs for each corner and cut linen 8 inches square. Finish same as for Center Mat.

BREAD AND BUTTER PLATE MATS (Make 4) . . . Make 3 motifs for each corner and cut linen 4 inches square. Finish same as for Center Mat.

GLASS MATS (Make 4) . . . Same as Bread and Butter Plate Mats.

Blossom Bread Tray Mat

MATERIALS:

CLARK'S O.N.T. or J. & P. COATS BEST SIX CORD MERCERIZED CROCHET, size 30, 1 ball of White, Ecru or any color.

A piece of linen 5 x 7 inches.

Completed doily measures about 5½ x 12¼ inches.

END . . . 1st rnd: Use shuttle and ball of thread. R of 3 ds, 3 p's sep. by 3 ds, 3 ds, cl. * Rw, ch of 4 ds, 4 p's sep. by 4 ds, 4 ds. Rw, r of 3 ds, join to p of adjacent r, 3 ds, p, 3 ds, p, 3 ds, cl. Repeat from * until there are 6 r's and 6 ch's, joining last p in 6th r to 1st p in 1st r, and joining 6th ch to base of 1st r. Tie and cut. 2nd rnd: R of 4 ds, p, 4 ds, join to 2nd p on ch of 1st rnd, 4 ds, p, 4 ds, cl. * Rw, ch of 6 ds, 3 p's sep. by 4 ds, 6 ds. Rw, r of 4 ds, p, 4 ds, join to 3rd p on same ch of 1st rnd, 4 ds, p, 4 ds, cl. Rw, r of 4 ds, p, 4 ds, join to 2nd p on next ch of 1st rnd, 4 ds, p, 4 ds, cl. Repeat from * around joining last ch to base of 1st r. Tie and cut. 3rd rnd: * R of 4 ds, 3 p's, sep. by 4 ds, 4 ds, cl. Rw, ch of 4 ds, join to 1st p on ch of 2nd rnd, 4 ds. Rw, r of 4 ds, join to p of adjacent r, 4 ds, p, 4 ds, p, 4 ds, cl. Rw, ch of 4 ds, join to center p of same ch of 2nd rnd, 4 ds. Rw, r of 4 ds, join to p of adjacent r, 4 ds, p, 4 ds, p, 4 ds, cl. Rw, ch of 4 ds, join to last p of same ch of 2nd rnd, 4 ds. Repeat from * around joining last p of 36th r to 1st p of 1st r, and fastening last ch to base of 1st r. This completes one end. Make another piece same as this.

SIDE EDGE . . . R of 4 ds, join to a free p on 3rd rnd of end, 4 ds, p, 4 ds, p, 4 ds, cl. * Rw, ch of 4 ds, p, 4 ds. Rw, r of 4 ds, join to last p of adjacent r, 4 ds, p, 4 ds, p, 4 ds, cl. Repeat from * until there are 24 r's and 24 ch's. Rw, r of 4 ds, join to last p of adjacent r, 4 ds, p, 4 ds, join to a free p on 3rd rnd of end, 4 ds, cl. Tie and cut. Finish other side to correspond leaving 20 r's free on outer edge of each end and 14 r's to be joined to the linen. Place lace on linen; draw a line lightly along inner edge of lace, having the line touch the p's. Cut linen to within ¼ inch of outline. Make a narrow hem all around, shaping corners as in illustration and having pencil mark at fold of hem. Sew lace to linen.

Ariel
Continued from page 51

2nd rnd: R of 3 ds, join to center p of last ch of one motif of 1st rnd, 3 ds, p, 3 ds, p, 3 ds, cl. Ch of 8 ds, p, 8 ds. Rw, r of 3 ds, 3 p's sep. by 3 ds, 3 ds, cl. Rw, ch of 8 ds, p, 8 ds. Make motif as in 1st rnd. Ch of 8 ds, join to p of opposite ch, 8 ds. Rw, r of 3 ds, 3 p's sep. by 3 ds, 3 ds, cl. Rw, ch of 8 ds, join to p of opposite ch, 8 ds. R of 3 ds, join to 3rd p of adjacent r, 3 ds, p, 3 ds, join to center p of first ch of next motif of 1st rnd, 3 ds, cl. Ch of 8 ds, join to 1st p of center ch of same motif of 1st rnd, 8 ds.

Rw, r of 3 ds, p, 3 ds, join to center p of adjacent r, 3 ds, p, 3 ds, cl. Rw, ch of 8 ds, p, 8 ds, make second motif, ch of 8 ds, join to p of opposite ch, 8 ds. Rw, r of 3 ds, 3 p's sep. by 3 ds, 3 ds, cl.

Rw, ch of 8 ds, skip 4 p's of same ch of same motif of 1st rnd, join to next p, 8 ds. R of 3 ds, join to center p of next ch of same motif of 1st rnd, 3 ds, p, 3 ds, p, 3 ds, cl. Continue around, making 16 points and joining last r and ch as in 1st rnd. Tie and cut. 3rd rnd: Work as for 2nd rnd, having 32 points.

BREAD AND BUTTER PLATE DOILY . . . Make 1st and 2nd rnds only.

GLASS DOILY . . . Make 1st rnd only.

Wild Rose Tray Mat

. . . **Materials:** CLARK'S O.N.T. or J. & P. COATS BEST SIX CORD MERCERIZED CROCHET, size 10, 3 balls of White or Ecru.

Completed doily measures about 12½ x 19 inches.

CENTER . . . Use shuttle and ball of thread. **First Medallion . . .** R of 2 ds, 5 p's sep. by 2 ds, 2 ds, cl. * Rw, ch of 4 ds, 4 p's sep. by 4 ds, 4 ds. Rw, r of 2 ds, p, 2 ds, join to 4th p of previous r, 2 ds, 3 p's sep. by 2 ds, 2 ds, cl. Repeat from *, joining 4th p of 6th r to 2nd p of 1st r. Join 6th ch to base of 1st r. Tie and cut.

Outer Motifs . . . R of 2 ds, 5 p's sep. by 2 ds, 2 ds, cl. Ch of 4 ds, p, 4 ds, join to 2nd p of ch of center, 4 ds, p, 4 ds. Rw. ** R of 2 ds, 5 p's sep. by 2 ds, 2 ds, cl. Rw, ch of 3 ds, p, 3 ds, join to 4th p of adjacent r, 3 ds, p, 3 ds. * Rw, r of 2 ds, p, 2 ds, join to 4th p of previous r, 2 ds, 3 p's sep. by 2 ds, 2 ds, cl. Rw, ch of 3 ds, 3 p's sep. by 3 ds, 3 ds. Repeat from * 4 more times.

Rw, make another r, joining 2nd and 4th p's to corresponding p's on adjacent r's (7 r's joined in circle). Rw, ch of 4 ds, p, 4 ds, join to 3rd p of same ch of center, 4 ds, p, 4 ds (one outer motif

completed). Rw, r of 2 ds, p. 2 ds, join to center p of adjacent ch of last outer motif, 2 ds, 3 p's sep. by 2 ds, 2 ds, cl. Rw, ch of 4 ds, p, 4 ds, join to 2nd p of next ch of center, 4 ds, p, 4 ds. Repeat from ** around, joining center p of last ch of 6th motif to 2nd p of 1st r made; make 7th r of 6th motif. Rw, ch of 4 ds, p, join to 3rd p of ch of center, 4 ds, p, 4 ds, join to base of 1st r made. Tie and cut. This completes first medallion.

Second Medallion . . . Make another medallion, joining center p's of 3rd and 4th chains on one outer motif to corresponding p's on first medallion. Tie and cut.

Third Medallion . . . Make another medallion, joining to second as second was joined to first, having 2 outer motifs free at both sides of center medallion, between joinings. This completes the center row (width of doily).

Fourth Medallion . . . Make another medallion, joining as before to outer

Continued on page 67

Rosebud Refreshment Set page 56

Wild Rose Tray Mat

54

Wild Rose Luncheon Set

Directions on page 56

Wild Rose Luncheon Set

Shown on page 55

. . . Materials: CLARK'S O.N.T. BEST SIX CORD MERCERIZED CROCHET, size 10, 20 balls of White or Ecru.

OR

J. & P. COATS BEST SIX CORD MERCERIZED CROCHET, size 10, 15 balls of White or Ecru.

1 yd. of linen, 36 inches wide.

This material is sufficient for a luncheon set consisting of 4 place mats and a center mat, each about 11½ x 17 inches, and 4 napkins about 14½ inches square.

PLACE MATS (Make 4) . . . First Medallion . . . Same as first medallion of Wild Rose Tray Mat on page 54.

Second Medallion . . . Make another medallion, joining center p of 4th ch of first outer motif to corresponding p of first medallion. Complete this motif, then join the center p of second free ch on next outer motif to corresponding p of first medallion. Complete medallion as before (no more joinings).

Third Medallion . . . Work as before, joining to previous medallion as second was joined to first. This completes one strip, which is width of place mat.

Fourth Medallion . . . Work as before, but join the center p's of 3rd and 4th ch's on one outer motif to corresponding p's on outer motif of first medallion, next to joining. Complete as before.

Fifth Medallion . . . Make another medallion, joining first outer motif to second medallion as fourth medallion was joined to first; then join the next 2 motifs to adjacent motifs of fourth medallion as second motif was joined to first. Make 3 x 4 medallions, joining as before.

FILL-IN MOTIF . . . R of 4 ds, p, 4 ds, join to center p of free ch on outer motif of a medallion and next to joining, 4 ds, p, 4 ds, cl. R of 4 ds, p, 4 ds, join to center p of free ch on next motif of same medallion, 4 ds, p, 4 ds, cl. Rw, ch of 10 ds, p, 10 ds, p, 10 ds. Rw, r of 4 ds, p, 4 ds, join to center p of next free ch on same motif of same medallion, 4 ds, p, 4 ds, cl. R of 4 ds, p, 4 ds, join to center p of free ch on next motif of adjacent medallion, 4 ds, p, 4 ds, cl. Rw, ch of 10 ds, join to 2nd p of ch, 10 ds, p, 10 ds.

Rw, r of 4 ds, p, 4 ds, join to center p of next free ch on same motif of same medallion, 4 ds, p, 4 ds, cl. R of 4 ds, p, 4 ds, join to center p of free ch on next motif of same medallion, 4 ds, p, 4 ds, cl. Rw, ch of 10 ds, join to 3rd p of ch, 10 ds. Rw, r of 4 ds, p, 4 ds, join to center p of free ch on next motif of adjacent medallion, 4 ds, p, 4 ds, cl. R of 4 ds, p, 4 ds, join to center p of next free ch on next motif of same medallion, 4 ds, p, 4 ds, cl. Rw, ch of 10 ds, join to p on ch where previous ch was joined, 10 ds, join to next p of ch where ch is already joined, 10 ds.

Rw, r of 4 ds, p, 4 ds, join to center p of free ch on same motif of same medallion, 4 ds, p, 4 ds, cl. R of 4 ds, p, 4 ds, join to center p of next free ch on next motif of next medallion, 4 ds, p, 4 ds, cl. Rw, ch of 10 ds, join to p on ch where ch's are already joined, 10 ds, join to next joining on ch, 10 ds. Rw, r of 4 ds, p, 4 ds, join to center p of next free ch on same motif, 4 ds, p, 4 ds, cl. R of 4 ds, p, 4 ds, join to center p of free ch on next motif, 4 ds, p, 4 ds, cl. Rw, ch of 10 ds, join to next joining on ch, 10 ds, join to base of 1st r. Tie and cut. This completes one fill-in motif. Fill in all other spaces in the same way.

CENTER MAT . . . Work exactly as for place mats.

NAPKINS (Make 4) . . . Corner . . . For center make r of 2 ds, 5 p's sep. by 2 ds, 2 ds, cl. * Rw, ch of 4 ds, 4 p's sep. by 4 ds, 4 ds. Rw, r of 2 ds, p, 2 ds, join to 4th p of previous r, 2 ds, 3 p's sep. by 2 ds, 2 ds, cl. Repeat from * 2 more times, joining 4th p of 4th r to 2nd p of 1st r, 2 ds, p, 2 ds, cl. Tie and cut.

Outer Motifs . . . R of 2 ds, 5 p's sep. by 2 ds, 2 ds, cl. Rw, ch of 3 ds, 3 p's sep. by 3 ds, 3 ds. Rw, r of 2 ds, p, 2 ds, join to 4th p of previous r, 2 ds, 3 p's sep. by 2 ds, 2 ds, cl. Rw, ch of 3 ds, 3 p's sep. by 3 ds, 3 ds. Rw, r of 2 ds, p, 2 ds, join to 4th p of previous r, 2 ds, 3 p's sep. by 2 ds, 2 ds, cl. Rw, ch of 4 ds, p, 4 ds, join to 2nd p of 1st ch of center, 4 ds, p, 4 ds.

Continued on page 67

Rosebud Refreshment Set

Shown on page 54

. . . Materials: CLARK'S O.N.T. BEST SIX CORD MERCERIZED CROCHET, size 30, 2 balls of White or Ecru, or 3 balls of any color.

OR

J. & P. COATS BEST SIX CORD MERCERIZED CROCHET, size 30, 2 balls of White, Ecru or any color.

This material is sufficient to make a large doily, about 7 inches square, and 6 glass doilies, each about 3¾ inches square.

GLASS DOILIES (Make 6) . . . Use shuttle and ball of thread.

First Motif . . . R of 7 ds, sm p, 3 ds, sm p, 7 ds, cl. Rw, ch of 5 ds, 3 p's sep. by 5 ds, 5 ds. * Rw, r of 7 ds, join to adjacent p of previous r, 3 ds, sm p, 7 ds, cl. Rw, ch of 5 ds, 3 p's sep. by 5 ds, 5 ds. Repeat from * once more. Rw, r of 7 ds, join to p of previous r, 3 ds, join to first p of first r, 7 ds, cl. Rw, ch of 5 ds, 3 p's sep. by 5 ds, 5 ds, join to base of 1st r. Tie and cut.

Second Motif . . . Work as for first motif, joining the 3rd p of one ch and the first p of following ch of second motif to corresponding p's on 2 ch's of first motif. Tie and cut.

Make 4 x 4 motifs, joining to adjacent motifs as second motif was joined to first, leaving center p free on corner chains of each motif.

LARGE DOILY . . . Make 7 x 7 motifs, joining as for glass doilies.

Shamrock Tray Mat

MATERIALS:

CLARK'S O.N.T. or J. & P. COATS BEST SIX CORD MERCERIZED CROCHET, size 30, 1 ball of White, Ecru or any color.

A piece of linen about 4 x 6½ inches finished with narrow hem all around.

Completed doily measures about 5 x 11½ inches.

END . . . Use shuttle and ball of thread. R of 3 ds, 3 p's sep. by 3 ds, 3 ds, cl (center r). Rw, ch of 6 ds, p, 6 ds. Rw, r of 3 ds, 3 p's sep. by 3 ds, 3 ds, cl. * Rw, ch of 6 ds, p, 6 ds. Rw, r of 6 ds, lp (¼ inch), 6 ds, cl. Rw, ch of 4 ds, 3 p's sep. by 4 ds, 4 ds. Rw, r of 6 ds, join to lp, 6 ds, cl. Rw, ch of 4 ds, 6 p's sep. by 2 ds, 4 ds. Rw, r of 6 ds, join to lp, 6 ds, cl. Rw, ch of 4 ds, 3 p's sep. by 4 ds, 4 ds. Rw, r of 6 ds, join to lp, 6 ds, cl. Rw, ch of 6 ds, join to p of opposite ch, 6 ds (a clover cluster). Rw, r of 3 ds, 3 p's sep. by 3 ds, 3 ds, cl. Rw, ch of 6 ds, join to p of opposite ch, 6 ds. Rw, r of 3 ds, join to p of adjacent r, 3 ds, p, 3 ds, p, 3 ds, cl (center r). Rw, ch of 6 ds, p, 6 ds. Rw, r of 3 ds, p, 3 ds, join to center p of opposite r, 3 ds, p, 3 ds, cl. Repeat from * until there are 5 clover clusters and there are 6 center r's. Tie and cut. This completes one end. Make another end same as this.

SIDE EDGE . . . Join thread to base of 3rd r on end clover. * Ch of 4 ds, 3 p's sep. by 4 ds, 4 ds. Rw, r of 6 ds, p, 6 ds. Repeat from * until there are 9 r's and 10 ch's. Tie securely to corresponding position on other end. Cut. Finish other side to correspond.

Jasmine

Primrose

58

Jasmine

MATERIALS:

CLARK'S O.N.T. or J. & P. COATS BEST SIX CORD MERCERIZED CROCHET, size 30.

SMALL BALL:

CLARK'S O.N.T.—13 balls of White or Ecru, or 17 balls of any color,

OR

J. & P. COATS —8 balls of White or Ecru, or 11 balls of any color.

BIG BALL:

J. & P. COATS —4 balls of White or Ecru, or 6 balls of any color.

This material is sufficient for a luncheon set consisting of a centerpiece about 15 inches in diameter, 4 place doilies about 12 inches in diameter, 4 bread and butter plate doilies about 7½ inches in diameter and 4 glass doilies about 4½ inches in diameter.

Use shuttle and ball of thread.

CENTERPIECE . . . 1st rnd: Starting at center make r of 3 ds, 3 p's sep. by 3 ds, 3 ds, cl. * Rw, ch of 5 ds, 4 p's sep. by 5 ds, 5 ds. Rw, r of 3 ds, join to adjacent p of previous r, 3 ds, p, 3 ds, p, 3 ds, cl. Repeat from * around until there are 10 r's joining last p of 10th r to adjacent p of 1st r. Join last ch to base of 1st r. Tie and cut. **2nd rnd:** R of 3 ds, p, 3 ds, join to 2nd p of any ch of 1st rnd, 3 ds, p, 3 ds, cl. * Rw, ch of 7 ds, p, 7 ds. Rw, r of 3 ds, p, 3 ds, join to 3rd p of same ch of 1st rnd, 3 ds, p, 3 ds, cl. Rw, ch of 7 ds, p, 7 ds. Rw, r of 3 ds, p, 3 ds, join to 2nd p of next ch of 1st rnd, 3 ds, p, 3 ds, cl. Repeat from * around, joining last ch to base of 1st r. Tie and cut (20 ch's). **3rd rnd:** R of 3 ds, p, 3 ds, join to p of any ch of 2nd rnd, 3 ds, p, 3 ds, cl. * Rw, ch of 8 ds, p, 8 ds. Rw, r of 3 ds, p, 3 ds, join to p of next ch of 2nd rnd, 3 ds, p, 3 ds, cl. Repeat from * around joining as before. Tie and cut. **4th rnd:** Same as 3rd rnd, but making ch's of 9 ds, p, 9 ds instead of 8 ds, p, 8 ds. **5th rnd:** R of 3 ds, p, 3 ds, join to p of any ch of 4th rnd, 3 ds, p, 3 ds, cl. * Rw, ch of 9 ds, p, 9 ds. Rw, r of 3 ds, p, 3 ds, join to same p where previous r was joined, 3 ds, p, 3 ds, cl (increase made). Rw, ch of 9 ds, p, 9 ds. Rw, r of 3 ds, p, 3 ds, join to p of next ch of 4th rnd, 3 ds, p, 3 ds, cl. Rw, ch of 9 ds, p, 9 ds. Rw, r of 3 ds, p, 3 ds, join to p of next ch of 4th rnd, 3 ds, p, 3 ds, cl. Repeat from * around, joining as before. Tie and cut (30 ch's). **6th rnd:** Same as 4th rnd. **7th rnd:** Same as previous rnd, but making ch's of 10 ds, p, 10 ds.

8th rnd: R of 3 ds, p, 3 ds, join to p of any ch of previous rnd which is directly above an increase on 5th rnd, 3 ds, p, 3 ds, cl. ** Rw, ch of 10 ds, p, 10 ds. Rw, r of 3 ds, p, 3 ds, join to same p where previous r was joined, 3 ds, p, 3 ds, cl. * Rw, ch of 10 ds, p, 10 ds. Rw, r of 3 ds, p, 3 ds, join to p of next ch of previous rnd, 3 ds, p, 3 ds, cl. Repeat from * 5 more times, then repeat from ** around (35 ch's). **9th rnd:** R of 3 ds, p, 3 ds, join to p of any increase ch of previous rnd, 3 ds, p, 3 ds, cl. Rw, ch of 10 ds, p, 10 ds. Mark this ch with colored thread. * Rw, r of 3 ds, p, 3 ds, join to p of next ch of previous rnd, 3 ds, p, 3 ds, cl. Rw, ch of 10 ds, p, 10 ds. Repeat from * around. **10th rnd:** R of 3 ds, p, 3 ds, join to p of marked ch of previous rnd, 3 ds, p, 3 ds, cl. * Rw, ch of 10 ds, p, 10 ds. Rw, r of 3 ds, p, 3 ds, join to p

Continued on page 67

Primrose

MATERIALS:

CLARK'S O.N.T. or J. & P. COATS BEST SIX CORD MERCERIZED CROCHET, size 30.

SMALL BALL:

CLARK'S O.N.T.—9 balls of White or Ecru, or 12 balls of any color,

OR

J. & P. COATS —6 balls of White or Ecru, or 8 balls of any color.

¾ yard of linen, 18 inches wide.

This material is sufficient for a luncheon set consisting of a centerpiece about 14½ inches in diameter, 4 place doilies about 10½ inches in diameter, 4 bread and butter plate doilies about 7½ inches in diameter, and 4 glass doilies about 5½ inches in diameter.

CENTERPIECE . . . 1st rnd: * Sr of 6 ds, cl. Rw, ch of 3 ds, 8 p's sep. by 3 ds, 3 ds. Rw. Repeat from * around until there are 28 sr's and 28 ch's. Join last ch to base of 1st sr, tie and cut. *Note*—These sr's do not show in photograph as they are covered by the linen.

2nd rnd: Fasten threads to 5th p of any ch of previous rnd. * Ch of 3 ds, 8 p's sep. by 3 ds, 3 ds, join to 4th p of next ch, 1 ds, lp, 1 ds, join to next p. Repeat from * around, joining end of last ch to beginning of 1st ch. Tie and cut. **3rd rnd:** * R of 4 ds, p, 4 ds, join to lp of previous rnd, 4 ds, p, 4 ds, cl. Rw, r of 4 ds, 4 p's sep. by 4 ds, 4 ds, cl. Rw, ch of 5 ds, join with shuttle thread to last p of last r, (5 ds, join with shuttle thread to next p) 3 times; 5 ds, join to base of r. Rw, ch of 7 ds, join with shuttle thread to space above last joining of previous ch, (7 ds, join to space above next joining) 3 times; 7 ds, join to base of r. Rw, ch of 9 ds, join to space above last joining of previous ch, 9 ds, join to space above next joining, 3 ds, p, 3 ds, p, 3 ds, (join to space above next joining, 9 ds) twice; join to base of r (rose made). Ch of 11 ds, join to 4th p of next ch of previous r, 8 ds. R of 4 ds, 4 p's sep. by 4 ds, 4 ds, cl. Ch of 8 ds, join to next p of same ch below, 11 ds. Rw. Repeat from * around, joining last ch to base of 1st r. Tie and cut. **4th rnd:** Fasten threads to 2nd p of any rose. * Ch of 3 ds, 8 p's sep. by 3 ds, 3 ds, join to 2nd p of next r on previous rnd, 1 ds, lp, 1 ds, join to next p of same r. Ch of 3 ds, 8 p's sep. by 3 ds, 3 ds, join to 1st p of next rose. Ch of 1 ds, lp, 1 ds, join to next p. Repeat from * around. Tie and cut. **5th and 6th rnds:** Same as 2nd rnd. Tie and cut. Place lace on linen and with a pencil draw a light line along inner edge of lace, having the line touch the bases of the sr's of 1st rnd. Hem linen, having the pencil mark at fold of hem. Sew lace to linen.

PLACE DOILIES (Make 4) . . . 1st rnd: Same as 1st rnd of centerpiece until there are 20 sr's and 20 ch's. Tie and cut. **2nd to 5th rnds incl:** Same as 2nd to 5th rnds incl of centerpiece. Tie and cut. Finish as for centerpiece.

BREAD and BUTTER PLATE DOILIES (Make 4) . . . 1st rnd: Same as 1st rnd of centerpiece until there are 16 sr's and 16 ch's. Tie and cut. **2nd to 4th rnds incl:** Same as 2nd to 4th rnds incl of centerpiece. Tie and cut. Finish as for centerpiece.

GLASS DOILIES (Make 4) . . . 1st rnd: Same as 1st rnd of centerpiece until there are 10 sr's and 10 ch's. Tie and cut. **2nd to 4th rnds incl:** Same as 2nd to 4th rnds incl of centerpiece. Tie and cut. Finish as for centerpiece.

Square Medallion
Placemat and Napkin

. . . MATERIALS: J. & P. Coats or Clark's O.N.T. Best Six Cord Mercerized Crochet, *Size 30, 1 ball.*

MOTIF . . . 1st rnd: R of (4 ds, sm p) twice; 4 ds, p, (4 ds, sm p) twice, 4 ds, cl and tie. * R of 4 ds, join to last sm p of preceding r, 4 ds, sm p, 4 ds, p, (4 ds, sm p) twice, 4 ds, cl, tie. Repeat from * 2 more times, joining the last sm p of the 4th r to the 1st sm p of the 1st r. Tie and cut. **2nd rnd:** Fasten ball and shuttle threads to 2nd sm p of 1st r of preceding rnd. * Ch of 5 ds, 3 sm p's sep by 5 ds, 5 ds and fasten to 3rd sm p of same r. Ch of 4 ds, p, 4 ds and fasten to 2nd sm p of next r of preceding rnd. Repeat from * around, fastening last ch to same sm p from which 1st ch started. Tie and cut. (For napkin, use only the 1st and 2nd rnds, making p's in 1st rnd instead of sm p's.) **3rd rnd:** Tie ball and shuttle threads together. * R of

10 ds, join to 1st sm p of ch on preceding rnd, 10 ds, cl. Rw, ch of 3 ds, 8 p's sep by 3 ds, 3 ds. Rw, r of 10 ds, join to 2nd sm p of same ch on preceding rnd, 10 ds, cl. Rw, make another ch like the preceding one. Rw, r of 10 ds, join to 3rd sm p on same ch of preceding rnd, 10 ds, cl. Skip p in short chain and repeat from * around, fastening the 12th r at the base of the 1st r. Tie and cut. **4th rnd:** Tie ball and shuttle threads together. With wrong side of work toward you, r of 9 ds, join to 3rd p in 1st ch of preceding rnd, * 7 ds, sm p, 2 ds, cl. R of 2 ds, join to sm p of preceding r, 7 ds, p, 9 ds, cl. Carry threads to sm p joining these 2 r's, fasten and make a ch of 9 ds, join to 6th p in same ch of preceding rnd, 4 ds. R of 6 ds, sm p, 3 ds, p, 9 ds, cl. Reversing curve of chain, ch of 3 ds, 15 p's sep by 3 ds, 3 ds. Rw, r of 9 ds, p, 3 ds, join to sm p of preceding r, 6 ds, cl. Reversing curve of ch, make a ch of 4 ds, join to 3rd p

of next ch on preceding rnd, 9 ds. Sp of 1/16 inch, rw, r of 2 ds, sm p, 7 ds, join to 6th p of same ch of preceding rnd, 9 ds, cl. Rw, r of 2 ds, join to sm p of preceding r, 7 ds, p, 9 ds, cl. Ch of 3 ds, 4 p's sep by 3 ds, 3 ds. R of 9 ds, join to 3rd p of next ch of preceding rnd. Repeat from * around, fastening the last ch at the base of the 1st 2 r's. Tie and cut.

The motifs are 3⅛ inches square. For each place mat, cut linen 13½ by 18½ inches; for each napkin, cut linen 12½ inches square. Hemstitch, making 1 inch hems. For place mat, with a sharp pencil draw 3¼ inch lines ¼ inch inside the hemstitching and parallel to each corner. Using these lines as guides, complete 3¼ inch squares in each corner and baste the motifs in place. Buttonhole stitch over the lines catching in the picots. Cut away the material from under the tatting. Finish napkins same as place mat on smaller scale required.

Doily measures
about 11½ x 6½ inches

Party Time Bread Tray Doily

MATERIALS:

J. & P. COATS or CLARK'S O.N.T. BEST SIX CORD MERCERIZED CROCHET, *Size 30,* 1 ball.

A piece of linen about 8½ x 6 inches.

There are seven points at each end of the doily.

1st Point . . . Starting at the inner edge of the shortest point, r of 3 ds, 3 p's sep. by 3 ds, 3 ds, cl. Rw, ch of 6 ds. Rw, r of 3 ds, 3 p's sep. by 3 ds, 3 ds, cl. Rw, ch of 4 ds, p, 4 ds. Rw, r of 3 ds, join to last p of preceding r, 3 ds, p, 3 ds, p, 3 ds, cl. Rw, ch of 5 ds, 3 p's sep. by 5 ds, 5 ds (this is end ch). Rw, r of 3 ds, p, 3 ds, join to 2nd p of opposite r, 3 ds, p, 3 ds, cl. Rw, ch of 4 ds, p, 4 ds. Rw, r of 3 ds, join to last p of preceding r, 3 ds, join to 2nd p of opposite r, 3 ds, p, 3 ds, cl. Rw, ch of 6 ds. Rw, r of 3 ds, p, 3 ds, join to 2nd p of opposite r, 3 ds, p, 3 ds, cl. This completes the 1st Point.

2nd Point . . . R of 3 ds, 3 p's sep. by 3 ds, 3 ds, cl. Ch of 6 ds. Rw, r of 3 ds, 3 p's sep. by 3 ds, 3 ds, cl. Rw, ch of 4 ds, join to p of adjacent ch in 1st Point, 4 ds. Rw, r of 3 ds, join to last p of preceding r, 3 ds, p, 3 ds, p, 3 ds, cl. Rw, ch of 5 ds, p, 5 ds. Rw, r of 3 ds, join to last p of preceding r, 3 ds, p, 3 ds, p, 3 ds, cl. Rw, ch of 6 ds, 3 p's sep. by 6 ds, 6 ds (this is end ch). Complete point in the same manner as the 1st Point, joining r's to those opposite.

3rd Point . . . R of 3 ds, 3 p's sep. by 3 ds, 3 ds, cl. Ch of 6 ds. Rw, r of 3 ds, 3 p's sep. by 3 ds, 3 ds, cl. Rw, ch of 4 ds, join to p of adjacent ch in preceding point, 4 ds. Rw, r of 3 ds, join to p of preceding r, 3 ds, p, 3 ds, p, 3 ds, cl. Rw, ch of 5 ds, join to p of adjacent ch of preceding point, 5 ds. Rw, r of 3 ds, join to p of preceding r, 3 ds, p, 3 ds, p, 3 ds, cl. Rw, ch of 6 ds, p, 6 ds. Rw, r of 3 ds, join to p of preceding r, 3 ds, p, 3 ds, p, 3 ds, cl. Rw, ch of 7 ds, 3 p's sep. by 7 ds,

7 ds. Complete point in the same manner as the preceding points.

4th Point . . . Same as the one just finished, except that you must join the 3rd ch to the adjacent ch of previous point.

5th Point . . . Same as the 4th Point.

6th Point . . . Work to correspond with 2nd Point.

7th Point . . . Work to correspond with 1st Point.

This completes the points at one end of doily. For the edge along the side, make r of 3 ds, 3 p's sep. by 3 ds, 3 ds, cl. Rw, * ch of 4 ds, 3 p's sep. by 4 ds, 4 ds. Rw, r of 3 ds, p, 3 ds, join to 2nd p of adjacent r of 3 ds, p, 3 ds, cl. R of 3 ds, 3 p's sep. by 3 ds, 3 ds, cl. Repeat from * until 13 ch's and pairs of r's are made.

Make the points for the other end as before, then continue with edging to correspond with opposite sides. Fasten last r at base of 1st r. Tie and cut.

Place lace on linen; draw a line lightly along inner edge of lace, having the line touch the p's. Cut linen to within ¼ inch of outline. Make a narrow hem all around, having pencil mark at fold of hem. Sew lace to linen.

Home Entertainment Coaster and Napkin

MATERIALS:

J. & P. COATS TATTING COTTON, 3 balls.

¼ yard linen, 36 inches wide.

This amount of material is sufficient for 6 coasters about 3½ inches in diameter and 6 napkins about 6 inches square.

COASTER . . . Starting at flower motif in the outside row, r of 3 ds, p, 4 ds, p, 4 ds, p, 3 ds, cl. Rw, ch of 5 ds, p, 5 ds, p, 5 ds. * Rw, r of 3 ds, p, 4 ds, join to 2nd p of 1st r, 4 ds, p, 3 ds, cl. Rw, ch of 5 ds, p, 5 ds, p, 5 ds. Repeat from * 2 more times. Fasten at base of 1st r. This completes

a flower. Ch of 9 ds, p, 3 ds. Rw, sr of 9 ds, p, 5 ds, p, 4 ds, cl. Rw, sr of 3 ds, join to p in preceding ch, 6 ds, p, 3 ds, p, 6 ds, cl. Rw, ch of 10 ds. Rw, lr of 12 ds, p, 12 ds, cl. Ch of 10 ds. Rw, sr of 6 ds, p, 3 ds, p, 6 ds, p, 3 ds, cl. Rw, sr of 4 ds, join to last p of 1st sr, 5 ds, p, 9 ds, cl. Ch of 3 ds, join to last p of the other sr, 9 ds. R of 3 ds, p, 4 ds, p, 4 ds, p, 3 ds, cl. Rw, ch of 5 ds, p, 5 ds, join to 1st p of last ch of corresponding flower motif, 5 ds. Rw and complete flower as before. Fasten at base of 1st r of flower.

Make 2 more groups same as this, but joining them to the preceding groups at the 2 p's of sr's and at the p of lr. These 3 groups make a half

circle. Make another half circle same as this.

Cut 6 circles of linen each 3 inches in diameter. Make a narrow hem around each piece and sew lace to linen along the edges.

NAPKIN . . . Make a flower for one corner and complete edging with r of 4 ds, join to adjacent p of flower, 4 ds, p, 4 ds, p, 4 ds, cl. * Sp ¼ inch. R of 4 ds, join to last p of preceding r, 4 ds, p, 4 ds, p, 4 ds, cl. Repeat from * until edging measures 20 inches, joining to flower at last p.

Cut 6 pieces of linen each 6 inches square. Cut off one corner of each napkin to fit flower of edging. Hem linen and sew lace to linen.

Victorian Tray Mat

. . . MATERIALS: J. & P.
COATS OR CLARK'S O.N.T. BEST SIX
CORD MERCERIZED CROCHET, *Size 30,
1 ball of White . . . A piece of linen
7 x 9 inches.*

END MOTIF . . . Beginning with the
3-r motif, r of 15 ds, (p, 5 ds) twice,
sm p, 5 ds, cl. R of 5 ds, join to sm p
of preceding r, 7 ds, p, 6 ds, p, 7 ds,
sm p, 5 ds, cl. R of 5 ds, join to sm p
of preceding r, (5 ds, p) twice, 15 ds,
cl. Make a spray as follows: Sp of ½
inch, r of 12 ds, p, 12 ds, cl. Rw, r of
12 ds, p, 12 ds, cl and tie over both
closings. Sp of ½ inch, rw, r of 11 ds,
p, 11 ds, cl. Rw, r of 11 ds, p, 5 ds, p,
6 ds, cl and tie. Sp of ⅜ inch, rw, r of

10 ds, p, 10 ds, cl. Rw, r of 5 ds, 3 p's
sep by 5 ds, 5 ds, cl and tie. Sp of ⅜
inch, rw, r of 9 ds, p, 9 ds, cl. Rw, r of
5 ds, p, 4 ds, p, 9 ds, cl. Sp of
¼ inch, r of 9 ds, p, 4 ds, p, 5 ds, cl,
tie and cut. Fasten thread to base of 3-r
motif and make another spray on the
other side to correspond. To complete
motif, r of 2 ds, p, 2 ds, join to 1st p
on 1st r of 3-r motif, 2 ds, join to p on
1st r of spray, (2 ds, join to p on adjacent r of spray) 3 times, 2 ds, p, 2 ds, cl.
Sp of ¼ inch, r of 2 ds, p, 2 ds, join to
last p of preceding r, (2 ds, p) twice,
2 ds, join to last p on last r of spray,
(2 ds, p) twice, 2 ds, cl. Sp of ¼ inch,
rw, r of 2 ds, 3 p's sep by 2 ds, 2 ds,
join to free p on 1st r of 3-r motif, 2 ds,

3 p's sep by 2 ds, 2 ds, cl. Sp of ¼ inch,
rw, r of 2 ds, p, 2 ds, join to last p of
next-to-last r, 2 ds, 5 p's sep by 2 ds,
2 ds, cl. Sp of ¼ inch, r of 2 ds, p, 2 ds,
join to last p of preceding r, 2 ds, 5 p's
sep by 2 ds, 2 ds, cl. Sp of ¼ inch, rw,
r of 2 ds, 3 p's sep by 2 ds, 2 ds, join
to 1st p on 2nd r of 3-r motif, 2 ds,
3 p's sep by 2 ds, 2 ds, cl. Sp of ¼ inch,
rw, r of 2 ds, p, 2 ds, join to last p of
next-to-last r, 2 ds, 5 p's sep by 2 ds,
2 ds, cl. Sp of ¼ inch, r of 2 ds, p, 2 ds,
join to last p on preceding r, 2 ds, 5 p's
sep by 2 ds, 2 ds, cl. Sp of ¼ inch, r of
2 ds, join to next-to-last p on preceding
r, 2 ds, 6 p's sep by 2 ds, 2 ds, cl. Sp of
¼ inch, rw, r of 2 ds, 3 p's sep by 2 ds,

Continued on page 68

Elegant Luncheon Set

MATERIALS:

CLARK'S O.N.T. or J. & P. COATS BEST SIX CORD MERCERIZED CROCHET, size 30.

SMALL BALL:

CLARK'S O.N.T.—40 balls of White or Ecru, or 50 balls of any color,

OR

J. & P. COATS —25 balls of White or Ecru, or 34 balls of any color.

BIG BALL:

J. & P. COATS —13 balls of White or Ecru, or 17 balls of any color.

This material is sufficient for a luncheon set consisting of 6 place mats, each 12 x 18 inches, and a center mat 16 x 38 inches.

CENTER MAT—First Motif . . . Use shuttle and ball of thread. Make lr of 5 ds, 3 p's sep. by 5 ds, 5 ds, cl. Rw, make a center r of 7 ds, p, 7 ds, cl. * Make a ch of 7 ds. Rw, r of 4 ds, join to adjacent p of lr, 4 ds, p, 4 ds, cl. Lr of 4 ds, join to p of adjacent r, 4 ds, p, 4 ds, p, 4 ds, cl. R of 4 ds, join to last p of lr, 4 ds, p, 4 ds, cl (a clover made). Rw, ch of 7 ds. R of 7 ds, join to p of center r, 7 ds, cl. Rw, lr of 5 ds, join to last p of clover, 5 ds, p, 5 ds, p, 5 ds, cl. Rw. Repeat from * until lr of 4th clover is completed. Then make r of 4 ds, join to last p of lr of clover, 4 ds, join to first p of first lr made at beginning of motif, 4 ds, cl. Rw, ch of 7 ds. Cut threads, leaving 3-inch lengths; tie to ends at beginning of motif and cut.

Second Motif . . . Work exactly as for 1st motif, joining one corner p to a corner p of 1st motif.

Third Motif . . . Join one corner to the corner p of second motif which is directly opposite joining between 1st and 2nd motifs. Continue in this way until there is a strip of 11 motifs.

First Motif of Second Strip . . . Holding first strip at top, join to 1st motif at left end of strip, by joining to the corner which is adjacent to the joining between 1st and 2nd motifs of first strip.

Second Motif of Second Strip . . . Join to motif just completed, joining one corner to 1st corner after previous joining, and joining next corner to adjacent corner of 2nd motif of 1st strip.

Continue to join motifs as before until there are 25 strips of 11 motifs each.

Fill in all spaces between motifs as follows: With shuttle make lr of 4 ds, p, 10 ds, join to p of lr at center of one side of motif, 10 ds, p, 4 ds, cl. * Lr of 4 ds, join to last p of previous r, 10 ds, join to free p on side of next motif, 10 ds, p, 4 ds, cl. Repeat from * once more. Lr of 4 ds, join to p of previous r, 10 ds, join to free p of next motif, 10 ds, join to free p of 1st lr of fill-in, 4 ds, cl. Cut and tie ends. Fill in all other spaces in same way.

PLACE MATS (Make 6) . . . Work exactly as for center mat, joining 8 strips of 12 motifs each. Complete as for center mat.

T-Square

MATERIALS:

CLARK'S O.N.T. or J. & P. COATS BEST SIX CORD MERCERIZED CROCHET, size 30.

CLARK'S O.N.T.—2 balls of White or Ecru, or 3 balls of any color.

OR

J. & P. COATS —2 balls of White, Ecru, or any color.

A linen tablecloth about 36 inches square, and 4 napkins about 12 inches square.

Use shuttle and ball of thread.

TABLECLOTH INSERTION (Make 4)—Flower . . . R of 3 ds, 3 p's sep. by 3 ds, 4 ds, sm p, 4 ds, lp, 4 ds, sm p, 4 ds, 3 p's sep. by 3 ds, 3 ds, cl. Rw, * ch of 3 ds, 6 p's sep. by 3 ds, 3 ds. Rw, r of 3 ds, 3 p's sep. by 3 ds, 4 ds, join to adjacent sm p, 4 ds, join to lp of 1st r, 4 ds, sm p, 4 ds, 3 p's sep. by 3 ds, 3 ds, cl. Repeat from * until there are 5 r's and 5 ch's, joining last r to adjacent sm p of 1st r, and last ch to base of 1st r. Tie and cut.

Continued on page 68

T-Square

Lacy Medallion Luncheon Set

Materials: Clark's O.N.T. or J. & P. Coats Mercerized Crochet, size 20 or 30; or Pearl Cotton, size 5. 1 shuttle and the ball.

Tumbler Doily: Center ring, 1 d s, 6 p's separated by 2 d s, 1 d s, close and tie. **1st rnd:** Tie ends of shuttle and ball threads. R, 3 d s, p, 3 d s, join to center ring, 3 d s, p, 3 d s, close. On ball thread make ch of 4 d s, p, 2 d s, p, 2 d s, p, 4 d s. (With the exception of the center ring, all rings and chs are the same throughout.) R, 3 d s, join to side ring, 3 d s, join to center ring, 3 d s, p, 3 d s, close. Make second ch same as first and continue around to form circle (6 rings). After each round is completed, tie off.

2nd rnd: R, 3 d s, p, 3 d s, join the 1st p of initial ch, 3 d s, p, 3 d s, close. On ball thread make ch of 4 d s, p, 2 d s, p, 2 d s, p, 4 d s. R, 3 d s, p, 3 d s, join to 3rd p of initial ch, 3 d s, p, 3 d s, close. Continue around to form circle (12 rings). **3rd rnd:** Attach rings to 1st and 3rd p of initial ch and only 1 ring to center p of next ch. Continue around circle making 18 rings with ch between each.

Salad Doily: Make first 3 rounds same as tumbler doily. **4th rnd:** Attach rings to 1st and 3rd p of initial ch and 1 ring to center p of the next 2 chs. Continue around circle making 24 rings and chs.

5th rnd: Attach rings to 1st and 3rd p of initial ch and 1 ring to center p of next 3 chs, making 30 rings and chs.

Bread and Butter Doily: Make first 5 rounds same as salad doily. **6th rnd:** Attach rings to 1st and 3rd p of initial ch, and 1 ring to center p of each of next 4 ch. Continue around circle making 36 rings with ch between each.

Plate Doily: Same as bread and butter doily for first 6 rounds. **7th rnd:** Attach rings to 1st and 3rd p of initial ch; 1 ring to center p of each of next 2 chs; 1 ring to 1st and 3rd p of 4th ch. Continue around circle making 48 rings with ch between each.

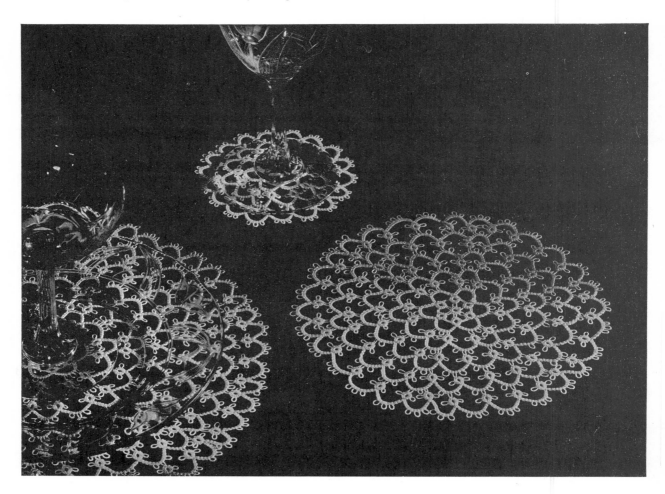

"Cutwork" Luncheon Set
Continued from page 49

* Rw, sp (3/8-inch). R of 4 ds, join to 1st p of adjacent r, 8 ds, p, 4 ds, p, 8 ds, cl. Rw, no sp. R of 4 ds, join to 1st p of adjacent r, 8 ds, p, 4 ds, p, 8 ds, cl. Insert tip of shuttle in sp to the right of 3/8-inch thread and fasten securely (as for joining to a p). Repeat from * until 14 rings are made (7 groups of 2 rings each). Sp (1/4-inch). R of 4 ds, join to adjacent p, 8 ds, p, 8 ds, join to adjacent p of r at opposite side, 4 ds, cl. Tie securely and cut. A spray is now made on one side. Skip 2 scallops of flower, attach shuttle

thread; and make a 2nd spray at right angle to 1st spray, joining first 2 rings of spray to next 2 p's of flower. This completes one corner motif.

Baste corners to linen, having outer edges of corners 1/2 inch in from hemstitching. With a ruler and pencil, draw a line around tatted corner, touching the p's. With Mercerized Crochet (or matching embroidery thread), work buttonhole stitch around the tatted corners and over the penciled line as for cutwork, making a stitch into each p to join lace to linen. Cut away linen at back of lace.

CENTER MAT . . . Cut a piece of linen 18½ x 36 inches. Make a 1¼-inch hem all around with hemstitching. Work and insert 4 corner motifs as for

place mats. Now make 2 more inserts as follows. Work as for corner motif until first spray is completed. Skip 4 scallops of flower, attach shuttle thread; make a second spray exactly opposite first spray. Baste one insert at center of long side of runner, ½ inch in from hemstitching, and finish as for corners. Sew second insert at opposite long side to correspond.

NAPKINS (Make 6) . . . Cut 6 pieces of linen, each 18 inches square. Make a ½-inch hem all around with hemstitching.

Napkin Insert: Work as for corner motif until first spray is completed. Baste lace insert on corner of napkin so that outer edge is ½ inch in from hemstitched edges, and finish as for other inserts.

Wild Rose Tray Mat
Continued from page 54

motif next to joining of first medallion, then join the following outer motif of fourth medallion to outer motif (next to joining) on second motif. Complete as before (no more joinings).

Fifth Medallion . . . Make another medallion and join as before to outer motifs next to joinings of fourth, sec-

ond and third medallions. Complete as before.

Sixth Medallion . . . Work as before, joining to outer motifs next to joinings of 4th and 5th medallions. Complete as before.

Seventh, Eighth and Ninth Medallions . . . Work and join to opposite side of center row of doily to correspond with joinings of 4th, 5th and 6th medallions. Tie and cut.

FILL-IN MOTIF . . . Fill in the 8 spaces between medallions as follows: R of 4 ds, p, 4 ds, join to center p of free ch on an outer motif, 4 ds, p, 4 ds, cl. R of 4 ds, p, 4 ds, join to center p of free ch on next motif, 4 ds, p, 4 ds, cl. Rw, ch of 10 ds, p, 10 ds. * (Rw, r of 4 ds, p, 4 ds, join to center p of free ch on next motif, 4 ds, p, 4 ds, cl) twice. Rw, ch of 10 ds, join to p of previous ch, 10 ds. Repeat from * once more. Join last ch to base of 1st r. Tie and cut.

Wild Rose Luncheon Set
Continued from page 56

* Rw, r of 2 ds, 5 p's sep. by 2 ds, 2 ds, cl. Rw, ch of 3 ds, p, 3 ds, join to 4th p of adjacent r, 3 ds, p, 3 ds. Rw, r of 2 ds, p, 2 ds, join to 4th p of previous r, 2 ds, 3 p's sep. by 2 ds, 2 ds, cl. Continue around until 7 r's and 6 ch's are made in circle, joining 4th p of the 7th r to the 2nd p of the 1st r. Rw, ch of 4 ds, p, 4 ds, join to next p of same

ch of center, 4 ds, p, 4 ds. Rw, r of 2 ds, p, 2 ds, join to center p of last ch on outer motif, 2 ds, 3 p's sep. by 2 ds, 2 ds, cl. Rw, ch of 4 ds, p, 4 ds, join to 2nd p of next ch of center, 4 ds, p, 4 ds. Repeat from * 2 more times. Then make 3 r's as in the beginning.

Cut linen to measure 14½ inches square. Place tatted piece over linen at corner, and mark off corner with a pencil. Cut away linen of corner, allowing a very small margin for a hem. Baste a very narrow hem around all edges of

napkin, and sew hem in place. Sew tatted corner in place by catching picots to the linen. Join threads to base of 1st r of corner, and make a ch of 3 ds, 3 p's sep. by 3 ds, 3 ds; with shuttle hook (or a fine crochet hook), draw loop from ball through linen, close to hem, pass shuttle through loop and finish as for a ds. Make chain-loops all around napkin, joining to linen at ½-inch intervals. Join last ch to base of last r of corner. Tie and cut.

Jasmine
Continued from page 59

of next ch of previous rnd, 3 ds, p, 3 ds, cl. Repeat from * 2 more times. *** Rw, ch of 10 ds, p, 10 ds. Rw, r of 3 ds, p, 3 ds, join to same p where previous r was joined, 3 ds, p, 3 ds, cl (increase made directly above increase on 5th rnd). ** Rw, ch of 10 ds, p, 10 ds. Rw, r of 3 ds, p, 3 ds, join to p of next ch of previous rnd, 3 ds, p, 3 ds, cl. Repeat from ** 6 more times, then repeat from *** around (40 ch's). 11th rnd: R of 3 ds, p, 3 ds, join to p of any ch of previous rnd which is directly above an increase on 8th rnd, 3 ds, p, 3 ds, cl. ** Rw, ch of 10 ds, p, 10 ds. Rw, r of 3 ds, p, 3 ds, join to same p where previous r was joined, 3 ds, p, 3 ds, cl. * Rw, ch of 10 ds, p, 10 ds. Rw, r of 3 ds, p, 3 ds, join to p of next ch of previous rnd, 3 ds, p, 3 ds, cl. Repeat from * 7 more times, then repeat from ** around (45 ch's). 12th rnd: R of 3 ds, p, 3 ds, join to p of any

ch of previous rnd, 3 ds, p, 3 ds, cl. * Rw, ch of 5 ds, 3 p's sep. by 5 ds, 5 ds, cl. Rw, r of 3 ds, p, 3 ds, join to p of next ch of previous rnd, 3 ds, p, 3 ds, cl. Repeat from * around.

EDGING . . . R of 6 ds, p, 6 ds, cl. Rw, ch of 6 ds, join to 1st p of any ch of previous rnd, 6 ds, p, 8 ds. Rw, r of 6 ds, join to p of previous r, 6 ds, cl. R of 5 ds, p, 5 ds, p, 5 ds, cl. * Rw, ch of 8 ds. Rw, r of 5 ds, join to adjacent p of last r, 2 ds, 4 p's sep. by 2 ds, 5 ds, cl. R of 5 ds, join to last p of previous r, 2 ds, 6 p's sep. by 2 ds, 5 ds, cl. R of 5 ds, join to last p of previous r, 2 ds, 4 p's sep. by 2 ds, 5 ds, cl. Rw, ch of 8 ds. Rw, r of 5 ds, join to last p of previous r, 5 ds, p, 5 ds, cl. R of 6 ds, p, 6 ds, cl. Rw, ch of 8 ds, join to p of adjacent ch, 6 ds, skip center p of ch of previous rnd, join to next p of same ch, 6 ds. Rw, r of 6 ds, join to p of last r, 6 ds, cl. Rw, ch of 6 ds, join to 1st p of next ch of previous rnd,

6 ds, p, 8 ds. Rw, r of 6 ds, join to same p where previous r was joined, 6 ds, cl. R of 5 ds, join to free p of next adjacent r, 5 ds, p, 5 ds, cl. Repeat from * around, joining last 2 r's to corresponding r's of 1st point, and joining last ch to base of 1st r made. Tie and cut (45 points).

PLACE DOILIES (Make 4) . . . 1st to 8th rnds incl: Same as 1st to 8th rnds incl of centerpiece. 9th rnd: Same as 12th rnd of centerpiece. Work edging as on centerpiece (35 points).

BREAD AND BUTTER PLATE DOILIES (Make 4) . . . 1st, 2nd and 3rd rnds: Same as 1st, 2nd and 3rd rnds of centerpiece. 4th rnd: Same as 12th rnd of centerpiece. Work edging as on centerpiece (20 points).

GLASS DOILIES (Make 4) . . . 1st rnd: Same as 1st rnd of centerpiece. Work edging as on centerpiece (10 points).

Victorian Tray Mat

Continued from page 63

2 ds, join to next p on 2nd r of 3-r motif, 2 ds, 3 p's sep by 2 ds, 2 ds, cl. Sp of ¼ inch, rw, r of 2 ds, join to next-to-last p on next-to-last r, 2 ds, 6 p's sep by 2 ds, 2 ds, cl. Sp of ¼ inch, r of 2 ds, join to next-to-last p on preceding r, 2 ds, 6 p's sep by 2 ds, 2 ds, cl. Sp of ¼ inch, rw, r of 2 ds, 3 p's sep by 2 ds, 2 ds, join to 1st p on 3rd r of 3-r motif, 2 ds, 3 p's sep by 2 ds, 2 ds, cl. Sp of ¼ inch, rw, r of 2 ds, join to next-to-last p of next-to-last r, 2 ds, p, 2 ds, join to last p on last r of spray, 2 ds, 4 p's sep by 2 ds, 2 ds, cl. Sp of ¼ inch, r of 2 ds, join to next-to-last p on preceding r, 2 ds, join to p on 7th r of spray, (2 ds, join to p on adjacent r of spray) 3 times, 2 ds, join to last p on 3rd r of 3-r motif, 2 ds, p, 2 ds, cl. Cut and tie. Make another End Motif the same way.

SIDE EDGE . . . Beginning with the 3-r motif, r of 4 ds, p, 8 ds, p, 4 ds, p, 4 ds, sm p, 4 ds, cl. R of 4 ds, join to

sm p of preceding r, 6 ds, p, 4 ds, p, 6 ds, sm p, 4 ds, cl. R of 4 ds, join to sm p of preceding r, 4 ds, p, 4 ds, p, 12 ds, cl. Sp of ¼ inch, r of 2 ds, p, 2 ds, join to 1st r of 1st r of 3-r motif, 2 ds, 5 p's sep by 2 ds, 2 ds, cl. * Sp of ⅜ inch, r of 2 ds, p, 2 ds, join to last p of preceding r, 2 ds, 5 p's sep by 2 ds, 2 ds, cl. Repeat from * until Side Edge measures 7¾ inches. Make another 3-r motif as follows: Sp of ¼ inch, r of 4 ds, join to next-to-last p of preceding r, 8 ds, (p, 4 ds) twice, sm p, 4 ds, cl. R of 4 ds, join to sm p of preceding r, 6 ds, p, 4 ds, p, 6 ds, sm p, 4 ds, cl. R of 4 ds, join to sm p of preceding r, (4 ds, p) twice, 12 ds, cl. Cut and tie. Make another strip the same way for the other side.

To join the End Motif to the Side Edge, r of 2 ds, p, 2 ds, join to 3rd p on 1st r of 3-r motif of Side Edge, 2 ds, 5 p's sep by 2 ds, 2 ds, cl. Sp of ¼ inch, r of 2 ds, p, 2 ds, join to last p of preceding r, 2 ds, 5 p's sep by 2 ds, 2 ds, cl. Sp of ¼ inch, r of 2 ds, p, 2 ds, join to last p of preceding r, 2 ds, p, 2 ds, join

to 1st p of 8th r of end spray, 2 ds, p, 2 ds, join to 1st p of adjacent r of same spray, 2 ds, p, 2 ds, cl. Sp of ¼ inch, rw, r of 2 ds, 5 p's sep by 2 ds, 2 ds, join to 1st p on 2nd r of 3-r motif of Side Edge, 2 ds, p, 2 ds, cl. Sp of ¼ inch, r of 2 ds, p, 2 ds, join to 2nd p of same r of 3-r motif, 2 ds, 5 p's sep by 2 ds, 2 ds, cl. Sp of ¼ inch, rw, r of (2 ds, p) twice, 2 ds, join to 3rd p of 6th r of spray, 2 ds, join to last p of adjacent r of spray, 2 ds, 3 p's sep by 2 ds, 2 ds, cl. Sp of ¼ inch, r of 2 ds, join to next-to-last p on preceding r, 2 ds, 6 p's sep by 2 ds, 2 ds, cl. Sp of ¼ inch and make another r the same way. Sp of ¼ inch, r of 2 ds, join to next-to-last p on preceding r, 2 ds, 4 p's sep by 2 ds, 2 ds, join to 1st p on 3rd r of Side Edge, 2 ds, p, 2 ds, cl. Cut and tie. Make 3 more joinings same as this.

Baste tatting to linen and mark linen with pencil just touching the picots on the inner edge. Buttonhole stitch over pencil-mark, catching in picots. Cut away material from under tatting.

T-Square

Continued from page 65

Stem and Leaves . . . Attach threads to 3rd p to left of any r of flower motif. Ch of 19 ds. Rw, r of 16 ds, join to 3rd p to right of same r of flower motif, 16 ds, cl. Rw, r of 16 ds, p, 8 ds, p, 8 ds, cl and tie over both closings. * Rw, ch of 14 ds, sr of 5 ds, sm p, 4 ds, cl. Ch of 14 ds. Rw, r of 16 ds, join to adjacent p of adjacent r, 16 ds, cl. Rw, r of 16 ds, p, 8 ds, p, 8 ds, cl and tie over both closings. Repeat from * once more. Rw,

ch of 14 ds, sr of 5 ds, sm p, 4 ds, cl. Ch of 14 ds. Rw, r of 16 ds, join to adjacent p of adjacent r, 14 ds, sm p, 2 ds, cl. R of 2 ds, join to sm p of last r, 14 ds, p, 14 ds, sm p, 2 ds, cl. R of 2 ds, join to sm p of last r, 14 ds, p, 16 ds, cl. Tie and cut. Make stem and leaves on other side of flower to correspond (see illustration).

Place lace on corner of tablecloth so that outer edges of lace are about 4 inches from edges of cloth. With a ruler and pencil draw a line lightly along edges of lace, having the lines touch the p's. Buttonhole stitch along pencil lines, catching the adjacent p's of lace. Cut out linen

under lace.

NAPKIN INSERTION (Make 4) . . . Work same as tablecloth insertion until 1 sr has been made on 1st spray, then work ch of 14 ds. Rw, r of 16 ds, join to adjacent p of adjacent r, 14 ds, sm p, 2 ds, cl. R of 2 ds, join to sm p of last r, 14 ds, p, 14 ds, sm p, 2 ds, cl. R of 2 ds, join to sm p of last r, 14 ds, p, 16 ds, cl. Tie and cut. Make stem and leaves on other side of flower to correspond (see illustration). Place lace on one corner of napkin only having outer edges of lace about 1 inch from edges of napkin. Finish same as on cloth.

EDGINGS, CORNERS
AND MEDALLIONS

Cutting Corners to Beauty

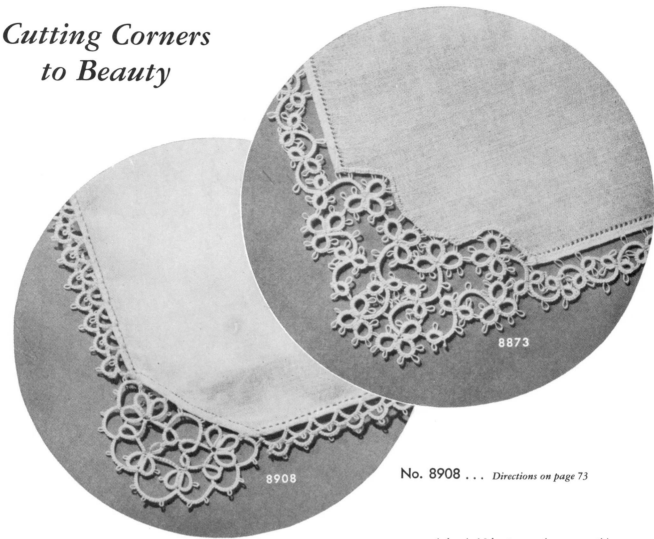

No. 8908 . . . *Directions on page 73*

No. 8873

MATERIALS:

J. & P. COATS TATTING COTTON, 1 ball.

Use 2 shuttles.

CORNER . . . Starting at the inside of one of the center sections, lr of 4 ds, 4 p's sep. by 4 ds, 4 ds, sm p, 4 ds, cl. Lr of 4 ds, join to sm p of preceding r, 4 ds, 3 p's sep. by 4 ds, 4 ds, sm p, 4 ds, cl. Lr of 4 ds, join to sm p of preceding r, 4 ds, 4 p's sep. by 4 ds, 4 ds, cl. Rw, ch of 8 ds, p, 4 ds, p, 8 ds. Rw, sr of 4 ds, 3 p's sep. by 4 ds, 4 ds, cl. Rw, make another r same as this. Rw, ch of 6 ds, p, 6 ds, p, 8 ds. Rw, lr of 4 ds, p, 4 ds, p, 4 ds, join to center p of 2nd sr, 4 ds, p, 4 ds, sm p, 4 ds, cl. Make 2 more lr's same as this to form a group of 3 as before. Tie and cut. To make corresponding section of corner, lr of 4 ds, p, 4 ds, p, 4 ds, join to next-to-last p of preceding r, 4 ds, p, 4 ds, p, 4 ds, sm p, 4 ds, cl. Lr of 4 ds, join to sm p of preceding r, 4 ds, 3 p's sep. by

4 ds, 4 ds, sm p, 4 ds, cl. Make another lr same as this. Rw, ch of 8 ds, join to p of preceding ch, 6 ds, p, 6 ds. Rw, sr of 4 ds, p, 4 ds, join to 2nd p of last r, 4 ds, p, 4 ds, cl. Rw, sr of 4 ds, p, 4 ds, join to center p of corresponding sr of 1st section, 4 ds, p, 4 ds, cl. Rw, ch of 8 ds, p, 4 ds, p, 8 ds. Rw, lr of 4 ds, p, 4 ds, p, 4 ds, join to corresponding p of 1st r of 1st section, 4 ds, p, 4 ds, sm p, 4 ds, cl. Lr of 4 ds, join to sm p of preceding r, 4 ds, 3 p's sep. by 4 ds, 4 ds, sm p, 4 ds, cl. Make 1 more lr of 4 ds, join to sm p of preceding r, 4 ds, 3 p's sep. by 4 ds, 4 ds, sm p, 4 ds, cl. Make 1 more lr same as this. Tie and cut.

* Next make the section that forms the outer edge of the corner. Sr of 4 ds, p, 4 ds, join to free single p of 1st of the 3 r's in the 2nd group of the 1st section, 4 ds, p, 4 ds, cl. Rw, ch of 6 ds, p, 6 ds. Rw, sr of 4 ds, p, 4 ds, join to 2nd p in 1st ch of 1st section, 4 ds, p, 4 ds, cl. Rw, sr of 4 ds, 3 p's sep. by 4 ds, 4 ds, cl. Rw, ch of 10 ds, p, 10 ds. Rw, lr of 4 ds, p, 4 ds, join to center p of preceding sr, 4 ds, p, 4 ds, p, 4 ds, sm p, 4 ds, cl. Lr of 4 ds, join to sm p of preceding r, 4 ds, 3 p's sep. by 4 ds, 4 ds, sm p,

4 ds, cl. Make 1 more lr same as this. Tie and cut. Repeat from * on opposite side, joining to corresponding picots.

To complete corner and start edging, lr of 4 ds, p, 4 ds, p, 4 ds, join to 2nd p of preceding r, 4 ds, p, 4 ds, sm p, 4 ds, cl. Lr of 4 ds, join to sm p of preceding r, 4 ds, p, 4 ds, join to 2nd p of 1st r made, 4 ds, p, 4 ds, sm p, 4 ds, cl. Lr of 4 ds, join to sm p of preceding r, 4 ds, 4 p's sep. by 4 ds, 4 ds, cl. Ch of 8 ds, p, 4 ds, p, 8 ds. Rw, sr of 4 ds, p, 4 ds, join to 3rd p of 2nd r in group of 3 r's in preceding outer-edge section, 4 ds, p, 4 ds, cl. Rw, ** sr of 4 ds, 3 p's sep. by 4 ds, 4 ds, cl. Rw, ch of 9 ds, p, 9 ds. Rw, sr of 4 ds, p, 4 ds, join to center p of preceding r, 4 ds, p, 4 ds, cl. Rw, sr of 4 ds, 3 p's sep. by 4 ds, 4 ds, cl. Rw, ch of 9 ds, p, 9 ds. Rw, sr of 4 ds, p, 4 ds, join to 2nd p of preceding r, 4 ds, p, 4 ds, cl. Repeat from ** around edge of handkerchief and complete corner to correspond.

Place lace corner on handkerchief, draw a line lightly along inner edge of lace, having the line touch the p's. Embroider with buttonhole stitch along the outline. Cut off excess linen and sew lace to linen. Sew remainder of edging to hem of handkerchief.

Beautiful Tatted Edgings

TRADITION

. . . Worked with Tatting Cotton, this edging will measure about 1 inch wide. Use shuttle and ball of thread. ** R of 4 ds, 3 p's sep. by 4 ds, 4 ds, cl. Rw, ch of 8 ds. Rw, sr of 4 ds, join to adjacent p of previous r, 4 ds, p, 4 ds, cl. Ch of 8 ds. Rw, r of 4 ds, 3 p's sep. by 4 ds, 4 ds, cl. * Sp (1/8-inch). R of 4 ds, join to adjacent p of previous r, 4 ds, p, 4 ds, p, 4 ds, cl. Repeat from * 3 more times. Rw, ch of 8 ds. Sr of 4 ds, join to free p of previous sr, 4 ds, p, 4 ds, cl. Rw, ch of 8 ds. Rw, r of 4 ds, join to free p of last sr, 4 ds, p, 4 ds, p, 4 ds, cl. Repeat from ** for desired length.

BUTTERFLY

. . . Worked with size 50 Mercerized Crochet, this edging will measure about 1 inch wide. Use two shuttles.

With 1st shuttle make a clover leaf as follows: R of 5 ds, 5 p's sep. by 5 ds, 5 ds, cl. * R of 5 ds, join to last p of previous r, 5 ds, 4 p's sep. by 5 ds, 5 ds, cl. Repeat from * once more (clover leaf made). Rw. Having 2nd shuttle thread over left hand, with 1st shuttle make ch of 10 ds. With 2nd shuttle make r of 7 ds, 3 p's sep. by 6 ds, 7 ds, cl. ** With 1st shuttle make a ch of 6 ds. With 2nd shuttle make r of 7 ds, join to last p of preceding r, 6 ds, p, 6 ds, p, 7 ds, cl. Repeat from ** once more. With 1st shuttle make ch of 10 ds. Rw. With 1st shuttle make r of 5 ds, p, 5 ds, p, 5 ds, join to center p of adjacent r of clover leaf, 5 ds, p, 5 ds, p, 5 ds, cl. Complete clover leaf as before. Rw. With 1st shuttle make ch of 10 ds. With 2nd shuttle make r of 7 ds, join to last p of adjacent r, 6 ds, p, 6 ds, p, 7 ds, cl. Continue in this manner for length desired. Tie and cut.

EMPRESS

. . . Worked with Tatting Cotton, this edging will measure about 1/2 inch wide. Use shuttle and ball of thread. R of 1 ds, 7 lp's sep. by 1 ds, 1 ds, cl. Rw, ch of 6 ds, lp, * 12 ds, lp, 6 ds, join to center p of last r, rw. Ch of 6 ds. R of 1 ds, 7 lp's sep. by 1 ds, 1 ds, cl. Rw, ch of 6 ds. Rw, r of 1 ds, 7 lp's sep. by 1 ds, 1 ds, cl. Rw, ch of 6 ds, join to adjacent p on p-ch. Repeat from * for desired length. Tie and cut.

WEDDING BELLS

. . . Worked with Tatting Cotton, this edging will measure about 1/2 inch wide. Use shuttle and ball of thread. Lr of 7 ds, p, 7 ds, cl. Rw, ch of 9 ds, p, 9 ds. * Rw, sr of 5 ds, join to p of lr, 5 ds, cl. Make 2 more sr's of 5 ds, p, 5 ds, cl, unjoined. Rw, ch like 1st chain. Rw, lr of 7 ds, join to p of last sr, 7 ds, cl. Lr of 7 ds, p, 7 ds, cl. Rw, ch like 1st ch. Repeat from * for length desired. Tie and cut. **2nd row:** Join threads to p of 2nd sr of previous row, * ch of 6 ds, p, 6 ds, join to p which joins lr to sr, ch of 3 ds, 5 p's sep. by 3 ds, 3 ds, join to p between next lr and sr. Ch of 6 ds, p, 6 ds, join to p of next sr. Repeat from * across. Tie and cut.

DIRECTIONS FOR FLEURETTE, DEBUT, FORSYTHIA ON PAGE 93

TRADITION

BUTTERFLY

EMPRESS

WEDDING BELLS

FLEURETTE

DEBUT

FORSYTHIA

CT-254

Butterfly Corner

MATERIALS: J. & P. Coats Tatting-Crochet, *Size 70, 1 ball of variegated color . . . 1 hemstitched linen handkerchief 11 inches square.*

Tie ball and shuttle threads together.

BUTTERFLY (Body) . . . Lr of 2 ds, 8 p's sep by 2 ds, 2 ds, cl. Rw, r of 8 ds, sm p, 8 ds, cl (head). Tie. Sp of 1/16 inch. Join to first p of lr, (ch of 5 ds, p, 5 ds, join to next p of same lr) 7 times. Turn. Ch of 7 ds, join to p of last picot chain, (ch of 5 ds, p, 5 ds, join to p of next ch) 6 times; ch of 7 ds, join to p of lr. Tie and cut. Attach thread to 3rd picot chain, ch of 3 ds. Rw, r of 10 ds, p, 10 ds, cl. Rw, ch of 15 ds, join to p of last r. Rw, r of 10 ds, p, 10 ds, cl. Rw, ch of 15 ds, sm p, 10 ds. Rw, r of 10 ds, join to p of last r, 10 ds, cl. Rw, r of 10 ds, p, 10 ds, cl. Rw, ch of 15 ds, join to p of last r. Rw, r of 5 ds, lp, 5 ds, cl. Rw, ch of 15 ds, join at base of next-to-last r, ch of 10 ds, sm p, 15 ds, skip 2 rings, join to p of the next r, ch of 15 ds, join at base of same r. Reverse curve of chain, ch of 3 ds, join to next picot chain. Tie and cut.

ANTENNAE . . . Sm r of 2 ds, sm p, 2 ds, cl. Rw, ch of 30 ds (to form slight curve), join to sm p of r of head. Reverse curve of chain, ch of 30 ds. Rw, sm r of 2 ds, sm p, 2 ds, cl. Tie and cut.

UPPER WING . . . Lr (same as for Body). Rw, lr. Tie. Sp of 1/16 inch, join to last p of preceding lr. Rw, (ch of 5 ds, p, 5 ds, join to next p of same lr) 7 times. Ch of 5 ds, p, 5 ds, join to first p of next lr. (Ch of 5 ds, p, 5 ds, join to next p of same lr) 7 times. Join to first picot chain of next lr. (Ch of 5 ds, p, 5 ds, join to next picot chain of same lr) twice. Ch of 5 ds, join to 2nd picot chain of Body, 5 ds, join to next picot chain of Upper Wing. Ch of 5 ds, join to next picot chain of Body, 5 ds, join to next picot chain of Upper Wing. (Ch of 5 ds, p, 5 ds, join to next picot chain of Upper Wing) 11 times. Tie and cut. Make opposite Upper Wing the same, joining to correspond.

LOWER WING . . . Lr (same as for Body). Sp of 1/16 inch, join to last p of lr. (Ch of 5 ds, p, 5 ds, join to next p of same lr) 7 times. Turn. Ch

of 7 ds, join to last picot chain of Lower Wing, ch of 5 ds, join to 2nd picot chain of Body (previously joined to Upper Wing), 5 ds, join to next picot chain of Lower Wing. Ch of 5 ds, join to next picot chain of Upper Wing, 5 ds, join to next picot chain of Lower Wing. (Ch of 5 ds, p, 5 ds, join to next picot chain of Lower Wing) 3 times. Ch of 5 ds, join to sm p of chain of Body, 5 ds, join to next picot chain of Lower Wing. Ch of 5 ds, p, 5 ds, join to p of lr of Lower Wing. Turn. Ch of 7 ds, join to last picot chain. Ch of 5 ds, join to 3rd joined picot chain of Body. Tie and cut. Make opposite Lower Wing the same, joining to correspond.

Sew in place. Cut away part of corner of Handkerchief (underneath lower wings), and make a narrow rolled hem.

EDGING . . . Tie ball and shuttle threads together. Attach to edge of handkerchief, close to Butterfly. * Ch of 5 ds, p, 5 ds, leaving sp of 3/8 inch on edge of linen and join to edge. Repeat from * around. Tie and cut.

Cutting Corners to Beauty

Shown on page 71

No. 8908

MATERIALS:

J. & P. Coats Tatting Cotton, 1 ball.

CORNER MOTIF . . . Starting at one of the 2 center rings, make r of 8 ds, p, 6 ds, p, 8 ds, cl. Rw, ch of 8 ds, p, 8 ds, p, 8 ds. Rw, r of 8 ds, join to 2nd p of preceding r, 6 ds, p, 8 ds, cl. Rw, ch of 6 ds. Rw, r of 8 ds, p, 6 ds, p, 6 ds, p, 8 ds, cl. R of 8 ds, join to last p of preceding r, 6 ds, p, 6 ds, p, 8 ds, cl. Make 1 more r same as this, joining to the preceding r as

before. Rw, ch of 6 ds. Rw, r of 8 ds, join to last p of preceding r, 6 ds, p, 8 ds, cl. Rw, ch of 6 ds. Rw, r of 8 ds, p, 8 ds, p, 8 ds, cl. Rw, ch of 6 ds. Rw, r of 8 ds, join to free p of 2nd r, 6 ds, cl. Rw, r of 8 ds, join to 2nd p of adjacent r, 8 ds, p, 8 ds, cl. Rw, ch of 9 ds. Rw, r of 8 ds, p, 8 ds, p, 8 ds, cl. Rw, sr of 6 ds, join to free p on 1st r. Rw, r of 8 ds, join to 2nd p of adjacent r, 8 ds, p, 8 ds, cl. Rw and work remainder of motifs to correspond, joining last ch of 6 ds to 1st r. Tie and cut.

Outer Row . . . Attach ball thread to free p on center r of 3-r group and make ch of 6 ds, p, 6 ds, p, 6 ds, join to adjacent r that has 1 free p; make 1 more ch as this, join to free p

of next r; make 1 more ch as before, join to joining-p of 2 r's; make center ch of 6 ds, 3 p's sep. by 6 ds, 6 ds, join to joining-p of next 2 r's and complete row to correspond with beginning. Tie and cut.

Cut off one corner of handkerchief (about 3/4 inch from point of corner) and hem. Sew lace corner to linen.

Edging . . . **1st row:** Fasten thread to edge of handkerchief, * ch of 5 ds, p, 2 ds, p, 2 ds, p, 5 ds, join to handkerchief, leaving 3/8 inch space. Repeat from * along entire edge. Tie and cut. **2nd row:** Attach thread to 1st p of 1st row. * Ch of 4 ds, p, 4 ds, join to 3rd p of same scallop. Ch of 2 ds, join to 1st p of next scallop. Repeat from * along entire edge.

Lacy Enchantment

J. & P. COATS
TATTING COTTON

8862

8880

Edgings for your daintiest lingerie,
your finest linens, your prettiest gifts

No. 8862 . . . R of 8 ds, sm p, 4 ds, p, 4 ds, p, 4 ds, sm p, 4 ds, cl. ** R of 4 ds, join to sm p of preceding r, 8 ds, p, 6 ds, sm p, 2 ds, sm p, 4 ds, cl. Carry thread on wrong side of work to the sm p joining the 2 r's and fasten but do not break off. Sp ½ inch. R of 2 ds, p, 2 ds, join to adjacent p of 1st r, 2 ds, 5 p's sep. by 2 ds, 2 ds, cl. * Sp ¼ inch. R of 2 ds, join to last p of preceding r, 2 ds, 6 p's sep. by 2 ds, 2 ds, cl. Repeat from * once more. Rw, sp ½ inch. R of 4 ds, sm p, 8 ds, join to free p of 2nd r, 6 ds, join to next sm p of 2nd r, 2 ds, sm p, 4 ds, cl. Rw, r of 4 ds, join to sm p of preceding r (catching in the ½-inch thread between the 5th and 6th r's to hold it in place), 4 ds, join to next-to-last p of 5th r, 4 ds, p, 4 ds, sm p, 8 ds, cl. Sp ⅜ inch. R of 8 ds, join to sm p of preceding r, 4 ds, p, 4 ds, p, 4 ds, sm p, 4 ds, cl. Repeat from ** for length desired.

No. 8880 . . . Make sr of 5 ds, sm p, 10 ds, sm p, 5 ds, cl.

Leaves . . . * Sp ⅜ inch. R of 8 ds, join to adjacent p of previous r, 7 ds, p, 3 ds, p, 12 ds, cl. R of 12 ds, p, 3 ds, p, 7 ds, sm p, 8 ds, cl and tie over both closings.

Flower . . . Sp ½ inch. R of 4 ds, sm p, 8 ds, join to last p of 1st leaf r, 8 ds, sm p, 4 ds, cl and tie. R of 4 ds, join to p of preceding r, 8 ds, p, 8 ds, sm p, 4 ds, cl and tie. Make 3 more r's same as one just made, then r of 4 ds, join to sm p of preceding r, 8 ds, join to 1st p of 2nd leaf r, 8 ds, join to sm p of 1st flower r, 4 ds, cl and tie. Carry thread to joining between 1st and 6th r's of flower and fasten. Carry thread to joining between the 2 leaf r's and fasten. Sp ⅜ inch. Make another sr of 5 ds, join to last p of 2nd leaf r, 10 ds, sm p, 5 ds, cl. Repeat from * for length desired, but joining the 2nd r to free p of 5th r of preceding flower.

No. 8869 . . . Starting at center flower, r of 3 ds, sm p, 9 ds, p, 9 ds, sm p, 3 ds, cl. * R of 3 ds, join to sm p of preceding r, 9 ds, p, 9 ds, sm p, 3 ds, cl. Repeat from * 3 more times, joining 4th r to sm p of 1st r. Tie and cut. Make several of these flowers and put aside to be used later. R of 4 ds, sm p, 8 ds, p, 12 ds, cl. ** Ch of 4 ds, 4 p's sep. by 4 ds, 4 ds. Rw, r of 12 ds, join to 2nd p of 1st r, 8 ds, sm p, 4 ds, cl. Rw, r of 9 ds, p, 3 ds, join to free p of 1st r of flower, 12 ds, cl. R of 12 ds, join to free p of 2nd r of flower, 12 ds, cl. Rw, ch of 4 ds, join to sm p of 2nd r, 4 ds, 4 p's sep. by 4 ds, 4 ds. Rw, r of 12 ds, join to same p of 2nd r of flower, 12 ds, cl. R of 12 ds, join to free p of 3rd r of flower, 12 ds, cl. Rw, ch of 4 ds, 6 p's sep. by 4 ds, 4 ds. Rw, r of 12 ds, join to same p of 3rd r of flower, 12 ds, cl. R of 12 ds, join to free p of 4th r of flower, 12 ds, cl. Rw, ch of 4 ds, 4 p's sep. by 4 ds, 4 ds, sm p, 4 ds. Rw, r of 12 ds, join to same p of 4th r of flower, 12 ds, cl. R of 12 ds, join to free p of 5th r of flower, 3 ds, p, 9 ds, cl. Rw, r of 4 ds, join to sm p of preceding ch, 8 ds, p, 12 ds, cl. Rw and repeat from ** for desired length.

Lucky Clover Edging

J. & P. COATS
TATTING COTTON

No. 8905 . . . Make all picots small and do not pull chain tight.

Ch of 4 ds, 8 p's sep. by 1 ds, 4 ds, p, 3 ds, p, 3 ds. Rw, r of 12 ds, p, 4 ds, p, 8 ds, cl. * R of 8 ds, join to 2nd p of preceding r, 8 ds, p, 8 ds, cl. R of 8 ds, join to p of preceding r, 16 ds, p, 8 ds, cl. Make another r like the 2nd r, then 1 r like the 1st. Rw, ch of 3 ds, join to last p of preceding ch, 3 ds, join to next p of same ch, 4 ds, 8 p's sep. by 1 ds, 4 ds, p, 3 ds, p,

3 ds. Rw, r of 12 ds, join to p of last r, 4 ds, p, 8 ds, cl. Repeat from * for length desired.

No. 8889 . . . Make all picots small. Starting with outer row, r of 7 ds, p, 7 ds, p, 7 ds, cl. * R of 7 ds, join to last p of preceding r, 7 ds, p, 7 ds, cl. Lr of 7 ds, join to p of preceding r, 7 ds, p, 7 ds, p, 7 ds, cl. R of 7 ds, join to last p of preceding r, 7 ds, p,

7 ds, cl. Rw, ch of 7 ds, p, 2 ds, join to last p of preceding r, 5 ds, p, 6 ds, p, 11 ds. Rw, r of 7 ds, join to free p of lr, 7 ds, p, 7 ds, cl. Repeat from * for length desired.

For the inner row, r of 4 ds, p, 5 ds, join to p of 1st ch, 4 ds, cl. * Rw, ch of 3 ds, 3 p's sep. by 1 ds, 3 ds, join to next p of 2nd ch, 3 ds, 3 p's sep. by 1 ds, 3 ds. Rw, r of 4 ds, join to next p of same ch, 5 ds, join to p of adjacent ch, 4 ds, cl. Repeat from * across.

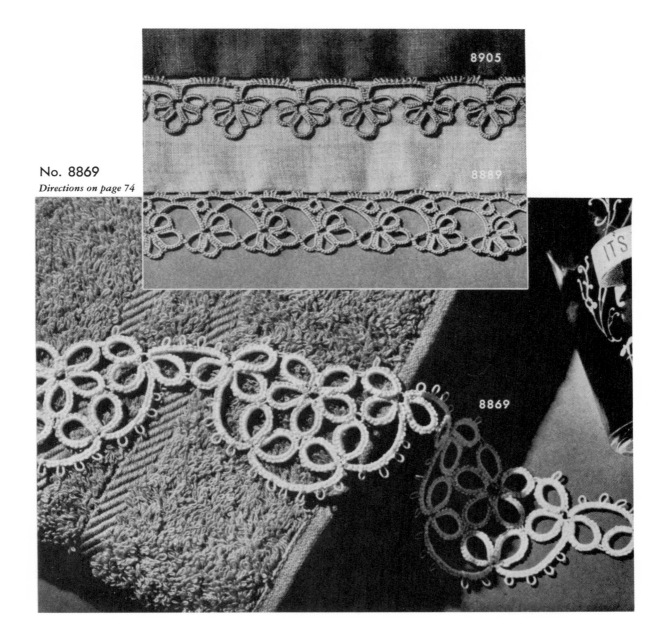

No. 8869

Directions on page 74

75

Edgings for Linens

No. 9079 . . . MATERIALS: J. & P. COATS TATTING COTTON, *Size 70.*

R of 9 ds, p, 7 ds, p, 2 ds, cl. * Rw, r of 9 ds, p, 3 ds, sm p, 6 ds, cl. Rw, sp of ¼ inch, r of 2 ds, join to 2nd p of next-to-last r, 2 ds, 9 p's sep by 2 ds, 2 ds, cl. Rw, sp of ¼ inch, r of 6 ds, join to sm p of next-to-last r, 3 ds, p, 9 ds, cl. Rw, r of 2 ds, join to last p of next-to-last r, 7 ds, p, 9 ds, cl. Rw, sp of ⅛ inch, r of 6 ds, cl. Rw, sp of ⅛ inch, r of 9 ds, join to p of next-to-last r, 7 ds, p, 2 ds, cl. Repeat from * for length desired. Tie and cut.

No. 9074 . . . MATERIALS: J. & P. COATS TATTING COTTON, *Size 70.*

1st row: Tie ball and shuttle threads together. * R of 2 ds, 4 sm p's sep by 2 ds, 4 ds, p, 4 ds, cl. Rw, ch of 9 ds, p, 9 ds, join to 4th sm p of preceding r. Rw and repeat from * for desired length, ending with a joined ch. Tie and cut. **2nd row:** Fasten ball and shuttle threads to 2nd sm p of 1st r of 1st row. Ch of 2 ds, sm p, 7 ds, sm p, 2 ds. * Join to 2nd sm p of next r on 1st row. Ch of 2 ds, join to sm p of preceding ch, 8 ds. Rw, r of 4 ds, (sm p, 4 ds) twice, join to 2nd sm p of next r on 1st row, (4 ds, sm p) twice, 4 ds, cl. Rw, ch of 22 ds. Rw, r of 4 ds, sm p, 4 ds, join to 3rd sm p of preceding r, 4 ds, join to same r to which preceding r is joined, (4 ds, sm p) twice, 4 ds, cl. Rw, ch of 8 ds, sm p, 2 ds, join to 2nd sm p of next r on 1st row. Ch of 2 ds, join to sm p of preceding ch, 7 ds, sm p, 2 ds. Repeat from * across. Tie and cut.

No. 9075 . . . MATERIALS: J. & P. COATS TATTING COTTON, *Size 70.*

Tie ball and shuttle threads together. R of 2 ds, 7 p's sep by 2 ds, 2 ds, cl. * Rw, ch of 6 ds, p, 6 ds. Rw, r of 2 ds, 7 p's sep by 2 ds, 2 ds, cl. Rw, ch of 6 ds, join to 6th p of next-to-last r, 5 ds, sm p, 1 ds. Rw, r of 7 ds, join to 6th p of preceding r, 3 ds, (p, 5 ds) twice, cl. Rw, r of 1 ds, join to sm p on preceding r, 9 ds, p, 9 ds, sm p, 1 ds, cl. Rw, ch of 1 ds, join to sm p of preceding r, 14 ds. Rw, r of (2 ds, p) twice, 2 ds, join to last p of next-to-last r, 2 ds, 4 p's sep by 2 ds, 2 ds, cl. Rw, ch of 14 ds, sm p, 1 ds. Rw, r of 5 ds, join to 5th p of preceding r, 5 ds, p, 3 ds, p, 7 ds, cl. Rw, r of 1 ds, join to sm p on preceding ch, 9 ds, p, 9 ds, sm p, 1 ds, cl. Ch of 1 ds, join to sm p of preceding r, 5 ds, p, 6 ds. Rw, r of 2 ds, p, 2 ds, join to last p of next-to-last r, 2 ds, 5 p's sep by 2 ds, 2 ds, cl. Ch of 6 ds, p, 6 ds. Rw, r of 2 ds, p, 2 ds, join to p on

next-to-last ch, 2 ds, 5 p's sep by 2 ds, 2 ds, cl. Repeat from * for desired length. Tie and cut.

No. 9077 . . . MATERIALS: J. & P. COATS TATTING COTTON, *Size 70.*

Tie ball and shuttle threads together. R of 3 ds, 6 p's sep by 3 ds, 3 ds, cl. Rw, ch of 1 ds, sm p, 7 ds, sm p, 2 ds. ** Rw, r of 6 ds, join to last p of preceding r, 2 ds, p, 8 ds, cl. Rw, r of 2 ds, join to sm p of preceding ch, 6 ds, p, 6 ds, sm p, 2 ds, cl. R of 2 ds, join to sm p of preceding r, 6 ds, p, 8 ds, cl and tie over closings of both r's (clover made). Rw, ch of 11 ds. R of 10 ds, p, 2 ds, sm p, 8 ds, cl. Ch of 9 ds, sm p, 3 ds. For round motif, rw, r of 7 ds, sm p, 3 ds, lp, 3 ds, sm p, 7 ds, cl. * Rw, ch of 3 ds, 4 p's sep by 3 ds, 3 ds. Rw, r of 7 ds, join to sm p of preceding r, 3 ds, join to lp of preceding r, 3 ds, sm p, 7 ds, cl. Repeat from * 2 more times. Rw, ch of 3 ds, 4 p's sep by 3 ds, 3 ds. Rw, r of 7 ds, join to sm p of preceding r, 3 ds, join to same lp, 3 ds, join to sm p of 1st r of round motif, 7 ds, cl. Rw, ch of 3 ds, p, 3 ds, join to free p of 3rd r of clover, (3 ds, p) twice, 3 ds. Join to base of 1st r of round motif, thus completing it. Ch of 3 ds, join to sm p of adjacent ch, 9 ds. R of 8 ds, join to sm p of adjacent r, 2 ds, p, 10 ds, cl. Ch of 11 ds. Rw, r of 8 ds, join to 3rd p on 1st ch of preceding round motif, 6 ds, sm p, 2 ds, cl. R of 2 ds, join to sm p of preceding r, 6 ds, p, 6 ds, sm p, 2 ds, cl and tie. Rw, r of 8 ds, p, 2 ds, p, 6 ds, cl (clover made). Rw, ch of 2 ds, join to sm p of next-to-last r, 7 ds, sm p, 1 ds. Rw, r of 3 ds, join to 2nd p of preceding r, 3 ds, 5 p's sep by 3 ds, 3 ds, cl. Rw, ch of 1 ds, join to sm p of preceding ch, 7 ds, sm p, 2 ds. Repeat from ** for length desired. Tie and cut.

No. 9080 . . . MATERIALS: J. & P. COATS TATTING COTTON, *Size 70.*

1st row: Sr of 2 ds, 5 sm p's sep by 2 ds, 2 ds, cl. Sp of ¼ inch, ** r of 5 ds, join to next-to-last sm p on preceding r, 5 ds, p, 5 ds, sm p, 5 ds, cl. Sp of ½ inch, make a flower as follows: R of 2 ds, sm p, 5 ds, join to sm p of preceding r, 5 ds, sm p, 2 ds, close to within 1/16 inch (this closing will be referred to as "part cl"). * R of 2 ds, join to last sm p of preceding r, (5 ds, sm p) twice, 2 ds, part cl. Repeat from * 2 more times. R of 2 ds, join to sm p of preceding r, 5 ds, sm p, 5 ds, join to 1st sm p of 1st r of flower, 2 ds, part cl. Join to base of 1st r of flower. Join thread to sm p joining 1st and 5th r's of flower. Sp of ½ inch, r of

5 ds, join to sm p of preceding r, 5 ds, p, 5 ds, sm p, 5 ds, cl. Sp of ¼ inch, r of 2 ds, sm p, 2 ds, join to sm p of preceding r, 2 ds, 3 sm p's sep by 2 ds, 2 ds, cl. Repeat from ** for length desired, ending with a sr. Now work along edge of 1st row as follows: **2nd row:** * Sp of ⅜ inch, join thread to sp at base of next r. R of 10 ds, sm p, 6 ds, cl and tie over closing, drawing thread through between the 2 sp-threads just preceding the r. Sp of ½ inch, r of 3 ds, join to sm p of preceding r, 7 ds, p, 7 ds, sm p, 3 ds, cl. Sp of ⅜ inch and join to base of next r of 1st row. R of 6 ds, join to sm p of preceding r, 10 ds, cl and tie. Sp of ⅜ inch and join to base of next sr. Repeat from * across. Tie and cut.

No. 9076 . . . MATERIALS: J. & P. COATS TATTING COTTON, *Size 70.*

1st row: Tie ball and shuttle threads together. ** Sr of 3 ds, 6 p's sep by 3 ds, 3 ds, cl. Rw, ch of 3 ds, 9 p's sep by 3 ds, 3 ds, sm p, 3 ds. Rw, sp of ⅛ inch, lr of 3 ds, sm p, 3 ds, 7 p's sep by 3 ds, 3 ds, sm p, 3 ds, cl. Lr of 3 ds, join to last sm p of preceding r, 3 ds, 7 p's sep by 3 ds, 3 ds, sm p, 3 ds, cl and tie to base of preceding r. Repeat from * once more. R of 3 ds, join to sm p of preceding r, 3 ds, 7 p's sep by 3 ds, 3 ds, join to 1st sm p of 1st lr, 3 ds, cl and tie to base of preceding r. Tie thread over the closing of 1st r to complete circle and carry thread to sm p joining the 1st and 4th lr's and fasten (clover made). Rw, ch of 3 ds, join to sm p of preceding ch, 3 ds, 9 p's sep by 3 ds, 3 ds (scallop complete). Rw, repeat from ** for length desired, ending with a sr and allowing 1½ inches for each scallop. Rw, ch of 3 ds, 12 p's sep by 3 ds, 3 ds. Now work along edge of 1st row as follows: **2nd row:** Rw, r of 4 ds, join to next-to-last p of last sr of 1st row, 6 ds, p, 3 ds, join to 4th p of adjacent r of next clover, 7 ds, cl. Rw, ch of 3 ds, 5 p's sep by 3 ds, 3 ds, join to 4th p of next r of same clover, * 3 ds, 9 p's sep by 3 ds, 3 ds, join to 4th p of next r of same clover, 3 ds, 5 p's sep by 3 ds. Rw, r of 7 ds, join to 4th p of next r of same clover, 3 ds, p, 6 ds, join to 2nd p of next sr, 4 ds, cl. Rw, ch of 3 ds, join to last p of preceding ch, (3 ds, p) twice, 3 ds. Rw, r of 4 ds, join to next-to-last p of next sr, 6 ds, p, 3 ds, join to 4th p of adjacent r of next clover, 7 ds, cl. Rw, ch of 3 ds, join to last p of preceding ch, 3 ds, 4 p's sep by 3 ds, 3 ds, join to 4th p of next r of same clover. Repeat from * across, ending with ch of 3 ds, join to last p of preceding ch, 11 p's sep by 3 ds, 3 ds. Tie to base of 1st sr made and cut.

Handwork of Beauty

J. & P. COATS TATTING COTTON

No. 8899 . . . R of 3 ds, 3 p's sep. by 3 ds, 3 ds, cl. Rw, ch of 6 ds, p, 6 ds. Rw, r of 3 ds, p, 3 ds, join to 2nd p of preceding r, 3 ds, p, 3 ds, cl. R of 3 ds, 3 p's sep. by 3 ds, 3 ds, cl. Rw, ch of 6 ds, p, 6 ds. * Rw, r of 3 ds, p, 3 ds, join to 2nd p of preceding r, 3 ds, p, 3 ds, cl. Make a ch as before, a r joining to same p as before, a ch, a r joining to same p. Then rw, r of 3 ds, 3 p's sep. by 3 ds, 3 ds, cl. Rw, ch of 6 ds, join to p on corresponding ch of adjacent group, 6 ds. Repeat from * for length desired.

No. 8866 . . . Two-Color Edging (Green and shaded Yellow). Use 2 shuttles, one wound with each color.

Directions for No. 8902 are on opposite page

Starting at flower, with Yellow shuttle, r of 3 ds, sm p, 12 ds, sm p, 3 ds, cl. R of 3 ds, join to p of preceding r, 12 ds, sm p, 3 ds, cl. R of 3 ds, join to last p of preceding r, 6 ds, sm p, 6 ds, sm p, 3 ds, cl. R of 3 ds, join to last p of preceding r, 4 ds, sm p, 8 ds, join to 1st p of 1st r, 3 ds, cl. Tie threads and clip off short end. To make Green stem, carry thread on wrong side of work to p between the 1st and 2nd r's of flower, fasten and attach Green shuttle thread to that same p. * Using the Green shuttle thread as a ball thread, make a ch of 18 ds.

To make 2nd flower, allow sp of ⅛ inch extra of Yellow thread and, using the Yellow shuttle, make another flower, following the directions for the 1st flower. Work with right side of tatting toward you and in joining last r to 1st, catch in the ⅛ inch of Yellow thread which you allowed in making the stem, to hold it in place.

To make Green leaf, carry Green shuttle thread to the center of the flower just completed, fasten and carry it to the p joining the 3rd and 4th r's. Fasten, turn work so that wrong side is toward you. With Green, r of 4 ds, join to adjacent p in 4th r of flower, 8 ds, join to free p of 3rd r in 1st flower, 3 ds, p, 15 ds, cl. Carry Green thread to center of flower, fasten and carry both threads to p joining the 1st and 2nd r's. Repeat from * for length desired.

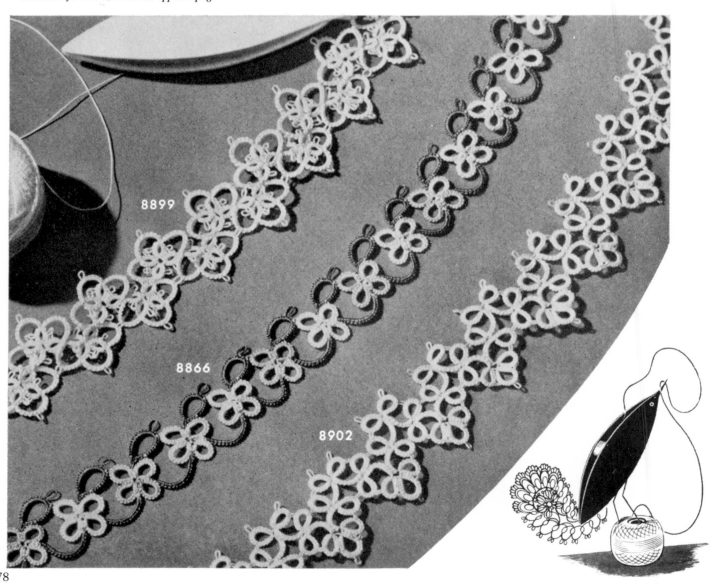

For Crisp Neckwear

J. & P. COATS TATTING COTTON

No. 8867 . . . * R of 6 ds, 3 p's sep. by 6 ds, 6 ds, cl. Rw, ch of 4 ds, 4 p's sep. by 4 ds, 4 ds. Rw, r of 6 ds, p, 6 ds, join to 2nd p of 1st r, 6 ds, p, 6 ds, cl. Rw, r of 6 ds, 3 p's sep. by 6 ds, 6 ds, cl. Rw, ch of 4 ds, 5 p's sep. by 4 ds, 4 ds. R of 6 ds, p, 6 ds, join to 2nd p of preceding r, 4 ds, p, 4 ds, sm p, 4 ds, cl. R of 4 ds, join to sm p of preceding r, 4 ds, 3 p's sep. by 4 ds, 4 ds, sm p, 4 ds, cl. R of 4 ds, join to sm p of preceding r, 4 ds, p, 4 ds, p, 6 ds, p, 6 ds, cl. Rw, ch of 4 ds, join to last p of preceding ch, 4 ds, 4 p's sep. by 4 ds, 4 ds. Rw, r of 6 ds, p, 6 ds, join to center free p of preceding r, 6 ds, p, 6 ds, cl. Rw and repeat from * for desired length.

No. 8861 . . . * R of 15 ds, sm p, 15 ds, cl. Make ch of 5 ds, 3 p's sep. by 5 ds, 5 ds. Join by shuttle thread to sm p of preceding r. Tie threads together to reverse their position. Rw, r of 12 ds, sm p, 3 ds, sm p, 15 ds, cl and join to p of 1st r. Rw, make another ch the same as the one just made and join to 2nd p of 2nd r. Rw, r of 3 ds, join to sm p of preceding r, 12 ds, p, 12 ds, sm p, 3 ds, cl and join to 2nd p of 2nd r. Make another r same as the one just made. R of 3 ds, join to sm p of preceding r, 12 ds, sm p, 15 ds, cl and join to p of 2nd r. Rw, ch of 5 ds, join to last p of preceding ch, 5 ds, p, 5 ds, p, 5 ds, join to p of preceding r. Rw, r of 15 ds, sm p, 15 ds, cl and join to p of preceding r. Rw, ch of 5 ds, 3 p's sep. by 5 ds, 5 ds and join to p of preceding r. Rw, r of 12 ds, sm p, 3 ds, sm p, 15 ds, cl and join to p of preceding r. Rw, make another ch same as the one just made and join to 2nd p of preceding r. Rw, r of 3 ds, join to sm p of preceding r, 12 ds, join to p of 3rd r of the group of 4 r's, 12 ds, sm p, 3 ds, cl and join to 2nd p of preceding r. R of 3 ds, join to sm p of preceding r, 12 ds, p, 12 ds, sm p, 3 ds, cl and join to p of 1st r of this group. R of 3 ds, join to p of preceding r, 12 ds, sm p, 15 ds, cl and join to p of 1st r of this group. Rw, ch of 5 ds, join to last p

of preceding ch, 5 ds, p, 5 ds, p, 5 ds and join to p of preceding r. Tie threads together to reverse their position. Rw and repeat from * for length desired.

No. 8902 . . . R of 6 ds, p, 5 ds, p, 6 ds, cl. Rw, ch of 8 ds. Rw, r of 6 ds, join to adjacent p of previous r, 5 ds, p, 6 ds, cl. Rw, r of 6 ds, p, 5 ds, p, 6 ds, cl. * Rw, ch of 8 ds. Rw, r of 6 ds, join to 2nd p of adjacent r, 5 ds, p, 6 ds, cl. Lr of 6 ds, join to adjacent p of preceding r, 5 ds, p, 5 ds, p, 6 ds, cl. R of 6 ds, join to adjacent p of preceding r, 5 ds, p, 6 ds, cl. Rw, ch of 8 ds. R of 6 ds, join to free p of adjacent r, 5 ds, p, 6 ds, cl. Rw, r of 6 ds, join to free p of adjacent r of 3-r group, 5 ds, p, 6 ds, cl. Rw, ch of 8 ds, r of 6 ds, join to free p of adjacent r, 5 ds, p, 6 ds, cl. R of 6 ds, p, 5 ds, p, 6 ds, cl. Rw, ch of 8 ds. Rw, r of 6 ds, join to adjacent p of preceding r, 5 ds, p, 6 ds, cl. Rw, r of 6 ds, join to free p of adjacent r, 5 ds, p, 6 ds, cl. Repeat from * for pattern.

Flower Garden Cluster

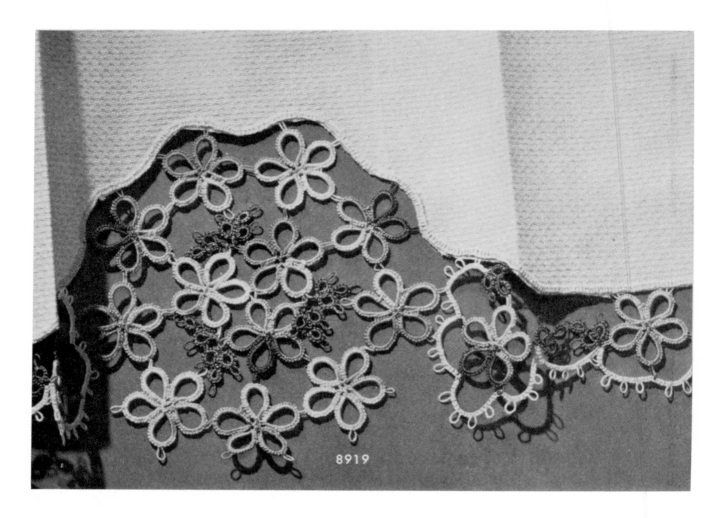

8919

No. 8919

MATERIALS:

J. & P. COATS TATTING COTTON, 1 ball each of White, Green, shaded Rose, shaded Yellow, and shaded Blue.

Toweling, 15 inches wide.

MEDALLION ... In making flowers, alternate colors for each flower. R of 5 ds, sm p, 10 ds, p, 10 ds, sm p, 5 ds, cl. R of 5 ds, join to last sm p of preceding r, 10 ds, p, 10 ds, sm p, 5 ds, cl. Make 3 more r's like one just made, joining the last r to the 1st sm p of 1st r. Tie and cut. This completes 1 flower.

To make the 3 flowers at the very center of Medallion, make another flower in same way joining 1 r to the p in one of the r's of the 1st flower. Make another flower and join it in the same way to the same p of the 1st flower.

There are 2 p's on each of these flowers which are so close to the cor-

responding p's of the adjacent flowers that they could almost be joined together. From these p's the green leaves are started.

LEAF ... All leaves are made in Green. Fasten Green shuttle thread to p of flower r, sr of 6 ds, p, 3 ds, sm p, 3 ds, cl. Sr of 3 ds, join to sm p of preceding r, 3 ds, p, 3 ds, p, 3 ds, cl and tie over both closings. Carry thread on wrong side to sm p and fasten. Sr of 5 ds, p, 5 ds, cl and fasten to same sm p. Carry thread back to base of first 2 r's, fasten. Fasten to p from which leaf started (1 leaf made); carry to adjacent p of next flower and fasten. Make another leaf in this p in same way joining this leaf to the previous one at p of adjacent r. Tie and cut. Make 2 more double leaves between flowers to correspond. Make a circle of 9 flowers around the 3-flower group joining flowers to each other at p's of adjacent r's so that there are 2 free petals on each flower on the outside of the circle *but* at the same time join 6 r's of inner circle to the

6 free r's of center 3-flower group leaving every 3rd r free.

EDGING ... Make 8 individual flowers. Make a leaf as before joining center r to a p on one of the 8 flowers just made. Using Green shuttle and a small ball (just a few yards) of White thread, make a ch of 4 ds, 3 p's sep. by 4 ds, 4 ds, join to p of upper r of one of the flowers of Medallion, 4 ds, p, 4 ds, join to next p of flower to which leaf is joined. Ch of 4 ds, p, 4 ds, join to p of next r of same flower of Medallion, 4 ds, p, 4 ds, p, 4 ds, join to next p of flower to which leaf is joined. Ch of 4 ds, 4 p's sep. by 4 ds, 4 ds, join to next p of same flower. Ch of 4 ds, 4 p's sep. by 4 ds, 4 ds, join to next p of same flower. * Rw, with shuttle make another leaf. Rw, ch of 4 ds, join to last p of preceding ch, 4 ds, 4 p's sep. by 4 ds, 4 ds. Rw, make another leaf joining center r to p of center r of adjacent leaf. Rw, join shuttle thread to a p in another flower.

Continued on page 81

Tip Your Towels with Tatting

No. 8812

MATERIALS:

J. & P. COATS TATTING COTTON, 1 ball each of White and Color.

A fingertip towel, 9 x 12 inches.

Wind shuttle with White. * R of 6 ds, p, 6 ds, cl. Rw, using ball of Color, ch of 6 ds, 3 p's sep. by 2 ds, 6 ds, rw. Repeat from * until 9 r's alternated by ch's are made. Rw, ch of 6 ds, 3 p's sep. by 2 ds, 6 ds, p, 6 ds. Rw, r of 6 ds, join to p of previous r, 6 ds, cl. Rw, ch of 6 ds. Rw, r of 6 ds, p, 6 ds, cl. Rw, ch of 6 ds. Rw, r of 6 ds, p, 6 ds, cl. Rw, ch of 6 ds, join to single p on opposite ch, 6 ds, 3 p's sep. by 2 ds, 6 ds. Rw, r of 6 ds, join to p of preceding r, 6 ds, cl. Rw, ch of 6 ds, 5 p's sep. by 2 ds, 6 ds. Rw, r of 6 ds, join to joining-p, 6 ds, cl. Rw, ch of 6 ds, 3 p's sep. by 2 ds, 6 ds, p, 6 ds. Rw, r of 6 ds, join to joining-p, 6 ds, cl. Rw, ch of 6 ds. Rw, r of 6 ds, join to p of opposite r, 6 ds, cl. Rw, ch of 6 ds. Rw, r of 6 ds, p, 6 ds, cl. Rw, ch of 6 ds, join to single p on opposite ch, 6 ds, 3 p's sep. by 2 ds, 6 ds. Rw, r of 6 ds, join to p of preceding r, 6 ds, cl. Work remainder of edging to correspond with other side. Tie and cut. Sew the p's on r's to edge of towel.

No. 8813

MATERIALS:

J. & P. COATS TATTING COTTON, 1 ball.

A fingertip towel, 9 x 12 inches.

* R of 4 ds, 3 p's sep. by 4 ds, 4 ds, cl. Rw, ch of 4 ds, 3 p's sep. by 4 ds, 4 ds. Rw. Repeat from * until 9 ch's alternated by r's are made. Rw, r of 10 ds, lp, 10 ds, cl. Rw, ch of 4 ds, p, 4 ds, join to 3rd p of adjacent r, 4 ds, p, 4 ds. ** Rw, r of 10 ds, join to lp, 10 ds, cl. Rw, ch of 4 ds, 3 p's sep. by 4 ds, 4 ds. Repeat from ** until a group of 6 r's are made. Rw, ch of 4 ds, 3 p's sep. by 4 ds, 4 ds. Rw, r of 4 ds, join to center p of next-to-last ch, 4 ds, p, 4 ds, p, 4 ds, cl. Work remainder of edging to correspond with other side. Tie and cut. Sew the p's on ch's to edge of towel.

No. 8919

Continued from page 80

Ch of 4 ds, join to last p of preceding ch, 4 ds, 3 p's sep. by 4 ds, 4 ds, join to next p of same flower. Make another ch and join to next p of flower. Repeat from * twice more.

The edging for the other side is made in the same manner and is joined to the opposite side of Medallion, leaving 3 flowers free at the bottom of Medallion.

Place tatting on towel and draw a line lightly along inner edge of lace having the line touch the p's and curving it slightly around center Medallion to form scallops. Embroider with buttonhole stitch along the outline catching in the p's. Cut out fabric under lace.

Handkerchiefs

No. 9066 . . . MATERIALS: J. & P. Coats Tatting Cotton, *Size 70, 1 ball.*

Sr of (4 ds, p) twice, 4 ds, cl and tie. * Rw, lr of 4 ds, 3 sm p's sep by 2 ds, 4 ds, sm p, 10 ds, cl and tie. Rw, sp of ¼ inch, r of 2 ds, join to 2nd p of sr, 2 ds, 6 p's sep by 2 ds, 2 ds, cl. Sp of ¼ inch and join thread to last sm p of lr. R of 4 ds, join to last p of preceding r, 4 ds, p, 4 ds, cl and tie. Repeat from * for length desired. Tie and cut.

No. 9063 . . . MATERIALS: J. & P. Coats Tatting Cotton, *Size 70, 1 ball . . . Handkerchief.*

MOTIF (Make 4) . . . Beginning at a corner, lr of 4 ds, sm p, 10 ds, p, 4 ds, p, 6 ds, sm p, 4 ds, cl. * Sr of 4 ds, join to last sm p of preceding lr, 2 ds, 9 p's sep by 2 ds, 2 ds, cl. Rw, sp of ³⁄₈ inch, make a center r of 8 ds, sm p, 4 ds, lp,

4 ds, sm p, 8 ds, cl. Rw, sp of ¼ inch, sr of (2 ds, p) twice, 2 ds, join to center p of preceding sr, 2 ds, 8 p's sep by 2 ds, 2 ds, cl. Rw, sp of ¼ inch, center r of 8 ds, join to last sm p of previous center r, 4 ds, join to lp of 1st center r, 4 ds, sm p, 8 ds, cl. Rw, sp of ³⁄₈ inch, sr of 2 ds, 4 p's sep by 2 ds, 2 ds, join to 2nd-from-last p of last sr, 2 ds, 4 p's sep by 2 ds, 2 ds, sm p, 4 ds, cl, join to sm p of preceding sr, 10 ds, p, 10 ds, sm p, 4 ds, cl. Sr of 4 ds, join to sm p of preceding r, 2 ds, 9 p's sep by 2 ds, 2 ds, cl. Rw, sp of ³⁄₈ inch, make and join another center r as before. Rw, sp of ¼ inch, r of (2 ds, p) twice, 2 ds, join to center p of last sr, 2 ds, 8 p's sep by 2 ds, 2 ds, cl. Rw, sp of ¼ inch, make and join another center r. Rw, sp of ³⁄₈ inch, r of 2 ds, 4 p's sep by 2 ds, 2 ds, join to 2nd-from-last p of last sr, 2 ds, 4 p's sep by 2 ds, sm p, 4 ds, cl. R of 4 ds, join to sm p of preceding r, 6 ds, p,

4 ds, p, 10 ds, sm p, 4 ds, cl. Repeat from * once more, joining the last sm p of last center r to 1st sm p of 1st center r and joining the last sm p of last sr to the 1st sm p of the 1st lr. Tie and cut.

EDGING . . . R of 2 ds, p, 2 ds, join to 2nd free p of 1st lr made on a motif, 2 ds, 5 p's sep by 2 ds, 2 ds, cl. * Sp of ¼ inch, r of 2 ds, p, 2 ds, join to next-to-last p of preceding r, 2 ds, 5 p's sep by 2 ds, 2 ds, cl. Repeat from * until piece reaches corresponding position on other side of handkerchief, joining 6th p on last r of edging to the 1st free p of 3rd lr made on next motif.

Continue thus until the 4 motifs are joined. After completing the tatting, baste the corners in place. With ruler, draw lines on handkerchief just touching the picots of the corner and fasten corners to handkerchief by buttonholing over this line, catching in the picots. Whip edging in place.

9066   9063

Delicate Tracery

9064

No. 9064 . . . MATERIALS: J. & P. Coats Tatting Cotton, *Size 70, 1 ball . . . Handkerchief.*

CORNER . . . First make the 5 flower motifs. R of 3 ds, sm p, 5 ds, p, 5 ds, sm p, 3 ds, cl. R of 3 ds, join to last sm p of preceding r, 5 ds, p, 5 ds, sm p, 3 ds, cl. Make 2 more r's the same way, joining the last sm p of the 4th r to the 1st sm p of the 1st r. Tie and cut—a small flower made. R of 4 ds, sm p, 6 ds, p, 6 ds, sm p, 4 ds, cl. Make 3 more r's same as this, joining them as r's of small flower were joined—a large flower made. Tie and cut. Make 3 more large flowers. Next make a scroll. Beginning at the inner corner, tie ball and shuttle threads together. R of 7 ds, join to p of 1st large flower, 5 ds, p, 12 ds, cl. Rw and, curving ch away from flower, make ch of 9 ds, p, 11 ds. Rw, r of 14 ds, join to p of 2nd large flower, 6 ds, cl. Join to p of small flower. Reversing curve of ch, ch of 14 ds, join to next p of small flower, r of 6 ds, join to next p of 2nd large flower, 14 ds, cl. Rw, ch of 9 ds. Rw, r of 12 ds, p, 12 ds, cl. R of 4 ds, sm p, 6 ds, cl. Tie and cut. Make another scroll to correspond on the other side of this piece, joining to next p on the 1st large flower, then joining the 1st ch of the 2nd scroll to the p in the 1st ch of the 1st scroll. Join 3rd large flower

to correspond with 2nd large flower. End by fastening the last ch of the 2nd scroll to the sm p of the last r on the 1st scroll. R of 12 ds, p, 12 ds, cl. Tie and cut.

SIDE SCROLL . . . R of (5 ds, p) twice, 10 ds, cl. Rw, ch of 18 ds and fasten to sm p between the 2 inner r's of the 2nd large flower. Carry thread on wrong side of work to the opposite p, fasten and make ch of 12 ds, p, 6 ds. Rw, r of 16 ds, cl. Rw, ch of 20 ds. Rw, r of 10 ds, p, 8 ds, sm p, 2 ds, cl. R of 2 ds, join to sm p of preceding r, 2 ds, (p, 4 ds) 3 times, cl. Rw, ch of 20 ds, sm p, 4 ds, sm p, 6 ds. R of 10 ds, p, 4 ds, join to 2nd p of 1st r of this scroll, 6 ds, cl. Tie and cut. Make another Side Scroll to correspond on other side. To complete corner, fasten ball and shuttle threads to sp at base of the r of 16 ds on the 1st Side Scroll. Ch of 20 ds. Rw, r of 4 ds, p, 4 ds, join to p in 2nd ch of Side Scroll, 4 ds, p, 2 ds, sm p, 2 ds, cl. R of 2 ds, join to sm p of preceding r, 8 ds, (p, 5 ds) twice, cl. Rw, ch of 20 ds. Rw, r of 4 ds, p, 4 ds, join to last p of preceding r, 4 ds, p, 2 ds, sm p, 2 ds, cl. R of 2 ds, join to sm p of preceding r, 4 ds, join to p on last r of 1st scroll, 4 ds, join to a p of the remaining large flower, 10 ds, cl. Rw, (ch of 20 ds, join to p in next r of

same flower) twice, ch of 20 ds. Rw, r of 10 ds, join to last p on same flower, 4 ds, join to p in last r of 2nd scroll, 4 ds, sm p, 2 ds, cl. R of 2 ds, join to sm p of preceding r, 2 ds, 3 p's sep by 4 ds, 4 ds, cl. Rw, ch of 20 ds. Rw, r of 5 ds, join to 2nd p of preceding r, 5 ds, p, 8 ds, sm p, 2 ds, cl. R of 2 ds, join to sm p of preceding r, 2 ds, p, 4 ds, join to p in 2nd ch of the Side Scroll, 4 ds, p, 4 ds, cl. Rw, ch of 20 ds, fasten at base of r of 16 ds. Tie and cut.

To complete the corner and start the edging, r of (5 ds, p) twice, 10 ds, cl. Ch of 4 ds, join to 2nd sm p of last ch of Side Scroll, 4 ds, join to 1st sm p of same ch, 20 ds. R of 10 ds, join to 2nd p of preceding r, 8 ds, sm p, 2 ds, cl. * R of 2 ds, join to sm p of preceding r, 2 ds, (p, 4 ds) 3 times, cl. Rw, ch of 20 ds. Rw, r of 5 ds, join to 2nd p of preceding r, 5 ds, p, 8 ds, sm p, 2 ds, cl. For edge, repeat from * for required length. Finish with a ch of 20 ds, join to sm p of Side Scroll, 4 ds, join to next sm p, 4 ds. R of 10 ds, join to p of preceding r, 5 ds, p, 5 ds, cl.

Baste corner to handkerchief, mark material with a pencil just touching picots and work buttonhole stitch over this line, catching in corresponding picots. Cut away material from under corner.

Edging No. 845
Medallions No. 830

Edging No. 8127
Medallion No. 8148

Edging No. 8132

Edgings and Medallions for Guest Towels

No. 845

Use J. & P. Coats Tatting Cotton.

* R of 5 ds, p, 5 ds, cl. Rw, sp (⅛-inch). R of 4 ds, p, 4 ds, p, 4 ds, p, 4 ds, cl. Rw, sp, lr of 5 ds, join to p of first r made, 3 ds, 5 p's sep. by 2 ds, 3 ds, p, 5 ds, cl. Rw, sp, r of 4 ds, join to 1st p of adjacent r, 4 ds, p, 4 ds, p, 4 ds, cl. Rw, sp, r of 5 ds, join to last p of lr, 5 ds, cl. Rw, sp, r of 4 ds, join to p of adjacent r, 4 ds, p, 4 ds, p, 4 ds, cl. Rw, sp. Repeat from * for length desired joining at 1st p of lr.

No. 830

Make r of 4 lp's sep. by 7 ds. Tie firmly and fasten off. **1st rnd:** Tie thread ends of shuttle and ball. * R of 4 ds, 8 p's sep. by 2 ds, 4 ds, cl. Rw, r of 4 ds, 5 p's sep. by 2 ds, 2 ds, join to p of center r, 2 ds, 5 p's sep. by 2 ds, 4 ds, cl. On ball thread make ch of 8 ds, 3 p's sep. by 1 ds, 8 ds. Rw, r of 6 ds, join to last p of r just made, 6 ds, cl. Rw and on ball thread make ch of 2 ds, p, 2 ds. Rw, r of 6 ds, p, 6 ds, cl. Rw and on ball thread make ch of 8 ds, 3 p's sep. by 1 ds, 8 ds. Repeat from * around, joining r's as shown in illustration. Fasten off.

No. 8132

Use one shuttle, a ball of thread and Milward's steel crochet hook.

With shuttle thread, sr of 5 ds, p, 4 ds, p, 4 ds, p, 5 ds, cl. * Lr of 5 ds, join to last p of sr, 5 ds, p, 1 ds, p, 1 ds, p, 5 ds, p, 5 ds, cl. Sr of 5 ds. join to p of lr, 4 ds, p, 4 ds, p, 5 ds, cl. Attach ball thread, rw, 11 ds, p, 11 ds, rw. With shuttle thread, sr of 5 ds, p, 4 ds, join to center p of sr, 4 ds, p, 5 ds, cl. Repeat from * for length desired. Break off. Attach thread to p on ch, and with crochet hook * ch 10, s c in p of next ch. Repeat from * across. Break off.

No. 8148

Materials: Clark's O.N.T. or J. & P. Coats Mercerized Crochet, size 30, 1 ball, and two shuttles.

When completed, medallion measures about 2¼ x 1½ inches.

Tie ball and shuttle threads together. In making the ch's, the 2nd shuttle thread is used the same as ball thread. With 1st shuttle, make r of 13 ds, p, 13 ds, cl. Rw, make 1st surrounding ch of 16 ds, join to p of r, p, 16 ds, join to base of r. 2nd surrounding ch of 6 ds, p, 6 ds, rw. With 2nd shuttle, make r of 5 ds, p, 4 ds, p, 4 ds, p, 5 ds, cl. Rw and continue ch of 5 ds. Rw and with 2nd shuttle make r of 5 ds, join to last p of 1st r, 4 ds, p, 4 ds, p, 5 ds, cl. Rw and continue ch of 5 ds, join to p of 1st ch. Rw, with 2nd shuttle make r of 5 ds, join to last p of 2nd r, 3 ds, p, 2 ds, p, 2 ds, p, 2 ds, p, 2 ds, p, 3 ds, p, 5 ds, cl. Rw and continue ch of 5 ds. Rw, with 2nd shuttle make r of 5 ds, join to last p of previous r, 4 ds, p, 4 ds, p, 5 ds, cl. Rw, continue ch of 5 ds. Rw, with 2nd shuttle make r of 5 ds, join to last p of previous r, 4 ds, p, 4 ds, p, 5 ds, cl. Rw and continue ch of 6 ds, p, 6 ds. Join to base of 1st surrounding ch. Make another ch of 5 ds. With 1st shuttle, make r of 13 ds, p, 13 ds, cl. Rw. Make 1st surrounding ch of 16 ds, join to p of r, p, 16 ds, join to base of r. Then make 2nd surrounding ch of 6 ds, join to last p of last surrounding ch of previous r's, 2 ds, 5 p's sep. by 2 ds, 3 ds, join to p of 1st surrounding ch, p, 3 ds, 6 p's sep. by 2 ds, 6 ds. Join to base of 1st surrounding ch. Make another ch of 5 ds (this completes one half of medallion). Repeat this half once more, joining at 1st and last p's of last surrounding ch. Fasten and break off.

No. 8127

Use one shuttle and a ball of thread. Tie ball and shuttle threads together. * Make r of 9 ds, p, 9 ds, cl. Rw, make surrounding ch of 14 ds, join to p of r, p, 14 ds, join to base of r. Make 2nd surrounding ch of 8 ds, p, 4 ds, p, 4 ds, p, 4 ds, join to p of 1st ch, p, 4 ds, p, 4 ds, p, 4 ds, p, 8 ds, join to base of 1st surrounding ch. Rw. Ch of 6 ds, p, 8 ds, p, 6 ds. Rw, r of 5 ds, p, 5 ds, join to last p of surrounding ch just made, 5 ds, p, 5 ds, cl. Make another r of 5 ds, 3 p's sep. by 5 ds, 5 ds, cl. Rw, ch of 6 ds, p, 8 ds, p, 6 ds. Repeat from * for length desired, joining 1st p of 2nd surrounding ch to center p of unjoined r.

No. 8145
(ILLUSTRATED BELOW)

Use one shuttle and a ball of thread. * Make lr of 5 ds, 5 p's sep. by 5 ds, 5 ds, cl. Make sr of 5 ds, p, 5 ds, p, 10 ds, cl. Rw. Make a ch of 5 ds, 4 p's sep. by 5 ds, 5 ds, join to last p of sr. Repeat from * for length desired. Tie securely, break off. This completes one half of insertion. Work other side of insertion as follows: ** Make lr of 5 ds, join to 1st p of lr on left, 5 ds, join to next p, 5 ds, join to p of sr, 5 ds, join to 1st p of next lr, 5 ds, join to next p of same lr, 5 ds, cl. Make sr of 5 ds, join to p of next lr, 5 ds, p, 10 ds, cl. Rw, make ch of 5 ds, 4 p's sep. by 5 ds, 5 ds, join to last p of sr just made. Repeat from ** across.

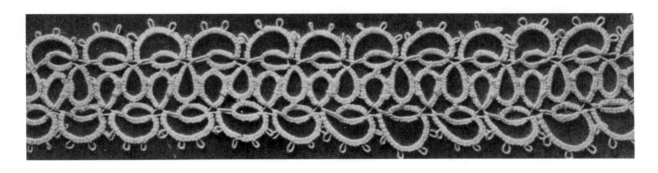

Scalloped Towel Edgings

No. 9104 . . . MATERIALS: J. & P. COATS TATTING COTTON, *Size 70, 2 balls of Shaded Greens and 1 ball each of Shaded Dark Blues, Shaded Dark Pinks and Shaded Yellows . . . A linen guest towel.*

FIRST MOTIF . . . Beginning with large flower in center of Motif, with Pink, make r of 5 ds, sm p, 7 ds, sm p, 3 ds, sm p, 10 ds, sm p, 5 ds, cl. R of 5 ds, join to last sm p of preceding r, 10 ds, sm p, 3 ds, sm p, 7 ds, sm p, 5 ds, cl. R of 5 ds, join to sm p of preceding r, 10 ds, sm p, 10 ds, sm p, 5 ds, cl. R of 5 ds, join to last sm p of preceding r, 7 ds, sm p, 3 ds, sm p, 10 ds, sm p, 5 ds, cl. R of 5 ds, join to last sm p of preceding r, 10 ds, sm p, 3 ds, sm p, 7 ds, sm p, 5 ds, cl. R of 5 ds, join to last sm p of preceding r, 10 ds, sm p, 10 ds, join to 1st sm p of 1st r, 5 ds, cl. Tie and cut. To make small flower, with Blue, make r of 4 ds, sm p, 8 ds, sm p, 4 ds, cl. R of 4 ds, join to 2nd sm p of 1st r, 8 ds, sm p, 4 ds, cl. R of 4 ds, join to sm p of preceding r, 4 ds, join to the single p of 3rd r of large flower, 4 ds, sm p, 4 ds, cl. R of 4 ds, join to sm p of preceding r, 8 ds, join to 1st sm p of 1st r of this flower, 4 ds, cl. Tie and cut. Make another small flower and join it in the same way to the 6th r of the large flower. Using Green for the edge of the Motif, tie ball and shuttle threads together. * R of 6 ds, join to p between 1st and 2nd r's of Blue flower (having wrong side of work uppermost), 6 ds, cl. Rw, ch of 3 ds, 5 p's sep by 3 ds, 3 ds. Rw, r of 9 ds, join to 1st free p of next free r of large flower, 3 ds, sm p, 6 ds, cl. Rw, ch of 3 ds, 3 p's sep by 3 ds, 3 ds. Rw, r of 6 ds, join to sm p of preceding r, 3 ds, join to next p of same r of large flower, 9 ds, cl. Rw, ch of 3 ds, 5 p's sep by 3 ds, 3 ds. Rw, r of 9 ds, join to next p of next r of large flower, 3 ds, sm p, 6 ds, cl. Rw, ch of 3 ds, 3 p's sep by 3 ds, 3 ds. Rw, r of 6 ds, join to sm p of preceding r, 3 ds, join to next p of same r of large flower, 9 ds, cl. Rw, ch of 3 ds, 5 p's sep by 3 ds, 3 ds. Rw, r of 6 ds, join to p between the 1st and 4th r's of the next Blue flower, 6 ds, cl. Rw, ch of 3 ds, 5 p's sep by 3 ds, 3 ds. Repeat from * once more, joining the last ch at base of 1st r.

SECOND MOTIF . . . Making large flower with Yellow, instead of Pink, work exactly the same as First Motif, joining them in center of next-to-last ch as follows: Ch of 3 ds, p, 3 ds, p, 3 ds, join to 3rd p of 5th ch of preceding motif, 3 ds, p, 3 ds, p, 3 ds.

Make necessary number of motifs, alternating colors of large flowers and joining them as Second was joined to First. Sew to edge of towel.

No. 9102 . . . MATERIALS: J. & P. COATS OR CLARK'S O.N.T. BEST SIX CORD MERCERIZED CROCHET, *Size 30.*

CENTER MOTIF . . . 1st rnd: R of 1 ds, 7 p's sep by 1 ds, 1 ds, cl. Leave thread ends long enough to form the 8th p, tie and cut. **2nd rnd:** Tie ball and shuttle threads together. R of 8 ds, sm p, 2 ds, join to p of center r, 2 ds, sm p, 8 ds, cl. * Rw, ch of 9 ds, p, 9 ds. Rw, r of 8 ds, join to last sm p of preceding r, 2 ds, join to next p of center r, 2 ds, sm p, 8 ds, cl. Repeat from * around, joining the 8th r to the 1st sm p

Continued on page 89

Dress Up Your Bath

No. 9085 . . . MATERIALS: J. & P. COATS OR CLARK'S O.N.T. PEARL COTTON, *Size 5, 2 balls . . . A Turkish towel.*

Tie ball and shuttle threads together. R of 4 ds, p, 8 ds, sm p, 12 ds, cl. Rw, ch of 3 ds, 5 p's sep by 3 ds, 3 ds. Fasten to sm p on preceding r. * R of 12 ds, sm p, 12 ds, cl. Rw, ch of (3 ds, p) twice, 3 ds. On outside of curve of ch make r of 7 ds, p, 5 ds, lp, 2 ds, sm p, 10 ds, cl. Continue ch with (3 ds, p) twice, 3 ds. Fasten to sm p on next-to-last r. R of 12 ds, sm p, 12 ds, cl. Rw, ch of 3 ds, 5 p's sep by 3 ds, 3 ds. Fasten to sm p on preceding r. R of 12 ds, p, 2 ds, sm p, 10 ds, cl. Rw, ch of (3 ds, p) twice, 3 ds. On outside curve of ch make r of 10 ds, join to sm p on 2nd-from-last r, 2 ds, join to lp on same r, 2 ds, sm p, 10 ds, cl. Continue ch with (3 ds, p) twice, 3 ds. Rw, r of 10 ds, join to sm p on next-to-last r, 2 ds, join to p on same r, 12 ds, cl. Rw, r of 12 ds, sm p, 12 ds, cl. Rw, ch of 3 ds, 5 p's sep by 3 ds, 3 ds. Fasten to sm p of preceding r.

R of 12 ds, sm p, 12 ds, cl. Rw, ch of (3 ds, p) twice, 3 ds. On outside of curve of ch make r of 10 ds, join to sm p of 3rd-from-last r, 2 ds, join to lp, 5 ds, p, 7 ds, cl. Continue ch with (3 ds, p) twice, 3 ds and fasten to sm p on next-to-last r. R of 8 ds, p, 4 ds, sm p, 12 ds, cl. Rw, ch of 3 ds, 5 p's sep by 3 ds, 3 ds. Fasten to sm p on preceding r. Rw, ch of 3 ds, p, 3 ds. R of 4 ds, p, 8 ds, sm p, 12 ds, cl. Rw, ch of 3 ds, join to last p on next-to-last ch, 3 ds, 4 p's sep by 3 ds, 3 ds and fasten to sm p on preceding r. Repeat from * for desired length. Sew to towel as illustrated.

No. 9096 . . . MATERIALS: J. & P. COATS OR CLARK'S O.N.T. PEARL COTTON, *Size 5, 1 ball each of Dusty Pink and Hunter's Green . . . A Turkish towel.*

FLOWER . . . With Pink, r of 4 ds, sm p, 8 ds, p, 8 ds, sm p, 4 ds, cl and tie. * R of 4 ds, join to last sm p of preceding r, 8 ds, p, 8 ds, sm p, 4 ds, cl and tie. Repeat from * 3 more times, joining the 5th r to the 1st sm p of the 1st r. Tie and cut. For a 16½-inch towel make 9 flowers.

LEAF . . . Tie Green ball and Green shuttle threads together. R of 3 ds, sm p, 1 ds, p, 1 ds, sm p, 3 ds, cl. Rw, ch of 6 ds, p, 1 ds, sm p, 1 ds and join to last sm p on preceding r. Ch of 1 ds, join to sm p on preceding ch, 4 ds, p, 4 ds, sm p, 1 ds and fasten to 1st sm p on preceding r. Ch of 1 ds, join to sm p of preceding ch, 1 ds, join to a p of a Flower, 6 ds and fasten at base of preceding r.

STEM . . . * Ch of 5 ds. Rw, r of 6 ds, p, 6 ds, cl. Rw, ch of 5 ds. Rw and make another Leaf, joining it to the p on the 2nd r of the same Flower. Rw, complete stem with ch of 10 ds, 5 p's sep by 2 ds, 10 ds. Make another Leaf just like the 1st, joining the 2nd ch to the p on the 2nd ch of the preceding Leaf. Repeat from * until all Flowers are joined.

Tatted Charm

Materials Required—AMERICAN THREAD COMPANY
"STAR" MERCERIZED TATTING COTTON,
ARTICLE 25

5—60 yd. Balls White.

1 Shuttle and 1 Ball.

4½ inch square of Linen.

Make a very narrow hem all around square.

1st Row. Using shuttle only, R, 3 d, 3 p sep by 3 d, 3 d, cl r. ⅛ inch space. ** Work a clover leaf at corner as follows: 3 d, join to last p of last r, 3 d, 2 p sep by 3 d, 3 d, cl r. LR, 3 d, join to last p of last r, 3 d, 3 p sep by 1 d, 3 d, p, 3 d, cl r. R, 3 d, join to last p of previous r, 3 d, 2 p sep by 3 d, 3 d, cl r. * ⅛ inch space. R, 3 d, join to last p of previous r, 3 d, 2 p sep by 3 d, 3 d, cl r. Repeat from * 20 times. Repeat from ** all around having 21 rings on each side between corners. Sew this 1st row to square of linen.

2nd Row. R, 3 d, p, 3 d, join to p of 1st r of clover leaf at corner, 3 d, p, 3 d, cl r. ⅛ inch space, turn. R, 3 d, 5 p sep by 2 d, 3 d, cl r, turn. Leave a ⅛ inch space between all rings in this row. R, 3 d, join to p of 1st r made 3 d, join to 1st p of large r of clover of 1st row, 3 d, p, 3 d, cl r, turn. R, 3 d, join to p of opposite r, 3 d, p, 3 d, p, 3 d, cl r. LR, 3 d, join to last p of last r, 2 d, 4 p sep by 2 d, 3 d, cl r. R, 3 d, join to last p of last r, 3 d, p, 3 d, p, 3 d, cl r, turn. R, 3 d, join to p of opposite r, 3 d, join to next

p of large r of clover, 3 d, p, 3 d, cl r, turn. R, 3 d, join to last p of opposite r, 2 d, 4 p sep by 2 d, 3 d, cl r, turn. R, 3 d, join to p of opposite r, 3 d, join to p of 3rd r of clover leaf, 3 d, p, 3 d, cl r, turn. * R, 3 d, join to last p of opposite r, 2 d, 4 p sep by 2 d, 3 d, cl r, turn. R, 3 d, join to last p of opposite r, 3 d, join to p of next r of 1st row, 3 d, p, 3 d, cl r, turn. Repeat from * across each side and work other corners to correspond.

3rd Row. With Shuttle and Ball, R, 4 d, 3 p sep by 4 d, 4 d, cl r. LR, 4 d, join to last p of last r, 4 d, 3 p sep by 2 d, 4 d, p, 4 d, cl r. R, 4 d, join to last p of last r, 4 d, 2 p sep by 4 d, 4 d, cl r turn. Ch, 5 d, 2 p sep by 2 d, 2 d, join to 1st free p of center r of clover of 2nd row, 5 d, turn. R, 4 d, p, 4 d, join to center p of last r made, 4 d, p, 4 d, cl r. LR, 4 d, join to last p of last r, 4 d, 7 p sep by 1 d, 4 d, p, 4 d, cl r. R, 4 d, join to last p of last r, 4 d, p, 4 d, p, 4 d, cl r, turn. Ch, 5 d, skip 1 p, join to next p of corner r of 2nd row, 2 d, 2 p sep by 2 d, 5 d, turn. R, 4 d, p, 4 d, join to center p of last r, 4 d, p, 4 d, cl r. LR, 4 d, join to last p of last r, 4 d, 3 p sep by 2 d, 4 d, p, 4 d, cl r. R, 4 d, join to last p of last r, 4 d, p, 4 d, p, 4 d, cl r, turn. Ch, 5 d, 2 p sep by 2 d, 2 d, skip last r of clover, join to center p of next r of 2nd row, 2 d, 2 p sep by 2 d, 5 d, turn. * Work another clover leaf joining to last clover leaf in same manner, turn. Ch, 5 d, 2 p sep by 2 d, 2 d, skip 1 r of 2nd row, join to center p of next r of 2nd row, 2 d, 2 p sep by 2 d, 5 d, turn. Repeat from * across sides and work corners same as 1st corner.

4th Row. R, 4 d, 3 p sep by 4 d, 4 d, cl r. LR, 4 d, join to last p of last r, 4 d, 3 p sep by 1 d, 1 d, join to 2nd free p of large r at corner of 3rd row, 1 d, 3 p sep by 1 d, 4 d, p, 4 d, cl r. R, 4 d, join to last p of last r, 4 d, 2 p sep by 4 d, 4 d, cl r turn. Ch, 6 d, 6 p sep by 1 d, 6 d, turn. R, 4 d, p, 4 d, join to center p of last r, 4 d, p, 4 d, cl r. LR 4 d join to last p of last r, 4 d, join to last free p of last large r, 1 d, 4 p sep by 1 d, 4 d, p, 4 d, cl r. R, 4 d, join to last p of last r, 4 d, p, 4 d, p, 4 d, cl r, turn. Ch, 5 d, 12 p sep by 1 d, 5 d, turn. R, 4 d, p, 4 d, join to center p of last r, 4 d, p, 4 d, cl r. LR, 4 d, join to last p of last r, 4 d, join to last p of last L r, 1 d, 4 p sep by 1 d, 4 d, p, 4 d, cl r. R, 4 d, join to last p of last r, 4 d, p, 4 d, p, 4 d, cl r, turn. Ch, 6 d, 6 p sep by 1 d, 6 d, turn. R, 4 d, p, 4 d, join to center p of last r, 4 d, p, 4 d, cl r. LR, 4 d, join to last p of last r, 4 d, join to last p of last large r, 1 d, 2 p sep by 1 d, 1 d, join to 4th free p of corner r of 3rd row, 1 d, 3 p sep by 1 d, 4 d, p, 4 d, cl r. R, 4 d, join to last p of last r, 4 d, p, 4 d, p, 4 d, cl r, turn. * Ch, 6 d, 6 p sep by 1 d, 6 d turn. R, 4 d, p, 4 d, join to center p of last r, 4 d, p, 4 d, cl r. LR, 4 d, join to last p of last r, 4 d, p, 2 d, join to center p of center r of next clover of 3rd row, 2 d, p, 4 d, p, 4 d, cl r. R, 4 d, join to last p of last r, 4 d, 2 p sep by 4 d, 4 d, cl r, turn. Repeat from * across side, work all corners in same manner.

5th Row. R, 4 d, 3 p sep by 4 d, 4 d, cl r. LR, 4 d, join to last p of last r, 4 d, 3 p sep by 2 d, 4 d, p, 4 d, cl r. R, 4 d, join to last p of last r, 4 d, p, 4 d, p, 4 d, cl r. Ch, 6 d, 2 p sep by 1 d, 1 d, join to 3rd p of 1st ch at corner of 4th row, 1 d, join to next p of same ch, 1 d, 2 p sep by 1 d, 6 d, turn. R, 4 d, p, 4 d, join to center p of last r, 4 d, p, 4 d, cl r. LR, 4 d, join to last p of last r, 4 d, 3 p sep by 2 d, 4 d, p, 4 d, cl r. R, 4 d, join to last p of last r, 4 d, 2 p sep by 4 d, 4 d, cl r. All clovers in this row are made in same manner, turn. Ch, 6 d, 2 p sep by 1 d, 1 d, skip 2 p of corner ch of 4th row, join in next p, 1 d, 2 p sep by 1 d, 6 d, turn. Work another clover, turn. Ch, 6 d, 2 p sep by 1 d, 1 d, skip 2 p of same ch of 4th row, join to next p, 1 d, 2 p sep by 1 d, 6 d, turn. Work another clover, turn. Ch, 6 d, 2 p sep by 1 d, 1 d, join to next p of same ch of 4th row, 1 d, 2 p sep by 1 d, 6 d, turn. Work another clover, turn. Ch, 6 d, 2 p sep by 1 d, 1 d, skip 2 p of same ch of

4th row, join in next p, 1 d, 2 p sep by 1 d, 6 d, turn. * Work another clover, turn. Ch, 6 d, 2 p sep by 1 d, 1 d, join to 3rd p of next ch of 4th row, 1 d, join to next p of same ch, 1 d, 2 p sep by 1 d, 6 d, turn. Repeat from * across sides and work all corners in same manner.

6th Row. R, 4 d, 3 p sep by 4 d, 4 d, cl r. LR, 4 d, join to last p of last r, 4 d, p, 2 d, join to center p of corner clover of 5th row, 4 d, p, 4 d, cl r. R, 4 d, join to last p of last r, 4 d, 2 p sep by 4 d, 4 d, cl r, turn. Ch, 6 d, 8 p sep by 1 d, 6 d, turn. R, 4 d, p, 4 d, join to center p of last r, 4 d, p, 4 d, cl r. LR, 4 d, join to last p of last r, 4 d, join to same center p of corner clover of 5th row, 2 d, p, 4 d, p, 4 d, cl r. R, 4 d, join to last p of last r, 4 d, 2 p sep by 4 d, 4 d, cl r, turn. * Ch, 6 d, 6 p sep by 1 d, 6 d, turn. R, 4 d, p, 4 d, join to center p of last r, 4 d, p, 4 d, cl r. LR, 4 d, join to last p of last r, 4 d, p, 2 d, join to center p of next clover of 5th row, 2 d, p, 4 d, p, 4 d, cl r. R, 4 d, join to last p of last r, 4 d, 2 p sep by 4 d, 4 d, cl r, turn. Repeat from * across side and work all corners in same manner.

7th Row. R, 4 d, 3 p sep by 4 d, 4 d, cl r. LR, 4 d, join to last p of last r, 2 d, 6 p sep by 2 d, 4 d, cl r. R, 4 d, join to last p of last r, 4 d, 2 p sep by 4 d, 4 d, cl r. Ch, 6 d, 2 p sep by 1 d, 1 d, join to 2nd p of corner ch of 6th row, 1 d, join to next p of same ch, 1 d, 2 p sep by 1 d, 6 d, p, 6 d, turn. R, 3 d, join to center p of last r, 3 d, p, 3 d, cl r, turn. Ch, 4 d, turn. R, 4 d, join to last p of last r, 2 d, 4 p sep by 2 d, 4 d, cl r. R, 4 d, join to last p of last r, 2 d, 6 p sep by 2 d, 4 d, cl r. R, 4 d, join to last p of last r, 2 d, 4 p sep by 2 d, 4 d, cl r, turn. Ch, 4 d, turn. R, 4 d, join to last p of last r, 4 d, p, 4 d, cl r, turn. Ch, 6 d, join to last p of opposite r, 6 d, 2 p sep by 1 d, skip 2 p of corner ch of 6th row, join to next p, 1 d, join to next p of same ch, 1 d, 2 p sep by 1 d, 6 d, turn. * R, 4 d, p, 4 d, join to last p of last r, 4 d, p, 4 d, cl r. R, 4 d, join to last p of last r, 2 d, 6 p sep by 2 d, 4 d, cl r. R, 4 d, join to last p of last r, 4 d, 2 p sep by 4 d, 4 d, cl r turn. Ch, 6 d, 2 p sep by 1 d, 1 d, join to 3rd p of next ch of 6th row, 1 d, join to next p of same ch, 1 d, 2 p sep by 1 d, 6 d, turn. Repeat from * across side and work all corners in same manner.

Scalloped Towel Edgings
Continued from page 86

of the 1st r and fastening the 8th ch at the base of the 1st r. Tie and cut. **3rd rnd:** R of 10 ds, join to p on ch of preceding rnd, 2 ds, sm p, 8 ds, cl. Rw, ch of 3 ds, sm p, 8 ds, p, 8 ds, sm p, 1 ds. * Rw, r of 8 ds, join to sm p of preceding r, 2 ds, join to same p on preceding rnd, 2 ds, sm p, 8 ds, cl. Rw, ch of 1 ds, join to sm p on preceding ch, 8 ds, p, 8 ds, sm p, 3 ds. Rw, r of 8 ds, join to sm p on preceding r, 2 ds, join to same p on preceding rnd, 10 ds, cl. R of 10 ds, join to p on next ch of preceding rnd, 2 ds, sm p, 8 ds, cl. Rw, ch of 3 ds, join to sm p on preceding ch, 8 ds, p, 8 ds, sm p, 1 ds. Repeat from * around, joining the last ch to the 1st sm p of the 1st ch and fastening threads at base of the 1st r. Tie and cut.

SIDE MOTIF . . . 1st rnd: Work same as 1st rnd of Center Motif. **2nd rnd:** R of 6 ds, sm p, 2 ds, join to p on center r, 2 ds, sm p, 6 ds, cl. * Rw, ch of 8 ds, p, 8 ds. Rw, r of 6 ds, join to sm p of preceding r, 2 ds, join to next p on center r, 2 ds, sm p, 6 ds, cl. Repeat from * around, joining the 8th r to the 1st sm p of the 1st r and fastening last ch at base of 1st r, but do not cut.

To complete, ch of 8 ds, p, 4 ds, p, 6 ds. Rw, r of 10 ds, join to p on 1st ch of preceding rnd, 8 ds, sm p, 2 ds, cl. R of 2 ds, join to sm p on preceding r, 8 ds, p, 10 ds, cl. Rw, ch of (7 ds, p) twice, 7 ds. Rw, r of 5 ds, join to p on a ch of Center Motif, 5 ds, p, 2 ds, sm p, 8 ds, cl. Rw, ch of 6 ds, join to p of next-to-last r, 6 ds, p, 6 ds. Rw, r of 8 ds, join to sm p of preceding r, 2 ds, join to p of same r, 2 ds, sm p, 8 ds, cl. Rw, ch of (6 ds, p) twice, 6 ds. Rw, r of 8 ds, join to sm p of preceding r, 2 ds, join to p of next-to-last r, 5 ds,

join to next p on Center Motif, 5 ds, cl. Rw, ch of 9 ds, p, 9 ds. Rw, r of 10 ds, join to last p on next-to-last ch, 10 ds, cl. Rw, r of 10 ds, sm p, 10 ds, cl. Rw, ch of 10 ds, skip 1 p on Side Motif, join to next p on Side Motif, 10 ds and fasten to sm p on preceding r. Rw, ch of 8 ds, p, 8 ds. Rw, r of 10 ds, join to next p on Side Motif, 2 ds, sm p, 8 ds. Rw, ch of 8 ds, p, 8 ds. Rw, r of 8 ds, join to sm p of preceding r, 2 ds, join to same p of Side Motif, 10 ds, cl. * Rw, ch of 8 ds, p, 8 ds. Rw, r of 10 ds, p, 2 ds, sm p, 8 ds, cl. Rw, ch of 8 ds, p, 8 ds. Rw, r of 8 ds, join to sm p of preceding r, 2 ds, join to p of same r, 10 ds, cl. Repeat from * for length required. Work other side to correspond.

Place tatting on end of towel and baste firmly to material. With a pencil, draw a line on the towel, just touching the picots. Buttonhole stitch over line catching in picots. Cut away fabric underneath.

Treasured Edgings

USE J. & P. COATS TATTING COTTON

No. 8822 . . . Sr of 5 ds, p, 5 ds, p, 5 ds, cl. * Rw, ch of 5 ds, p, 5 ds. Rw, lr of 14 ds, p, 14 ds, cl. Ch of 9 ds, join to adjacent p of sr, 3 ds, p, 3 ds, p, 3 ds, join to p of lr, 3 p's sep. by 3 ds, 9 ds. Join to base of lr (double r made). Rw, ch of 5 ds, p, 5 ds. Rw, sr of 5 ds, join to adjacent p of double r, 5 ds, p, 5 ds, cl. Repeat from * for desired length.

No. 8823 . . . Lr of 14 ds, p, 14 ds, cl. Rw, ch of 3 ds, 4 p's sep. by 3 ds, 3 ds, attach to p of lr, ch of 5 p's sep. by 3 ds, 3 ds, attach to base of lr (double r made). Ch of 5 ds, p, 5 ds. * Rw, sr of 5 ds, join to 1st p of ch around lr, 5 ds, cl. Rw, ch of 2 ds, 3 p's sep. by 2 ds, 2 ds. Rw, sr of 5 ds, attach to next p of ch around lr, 5 ds, cl. Rw, ch of 2 ds, 4 p's sep. by 2 ds, 2 ds. Rw, sr of 5 ds, join to next p, 5 ds, cl. Rw, ch of 2 ds, 3 p's sep. by 2 ds, 2 ds. Rw, sr of 5 ds, join to next p, 5 ds, cl. Rw, ch of 5 ds, p, 5 ds, join to next p (motif completed). Rw, ch of 6 ds, p, 6 ds. Make a double r as before, ch of 5 ds, join to p of corresponding ch of previous motif. Repeat from * for length desired.

No. 8436 . . . Use shuttle and ball of thread. R of 5 ds, p, 3 ds, 3 p's sep. by 2 ds, 3 ds, p, 5 ds, cl. Ch of 5 ds. R of 5 ds, join to last p of previous r, 3 ds, 3 p's sep. by 2 ds, 3 ds, p, 5 ds, cl. Rw, r of 5 ds, p, 3 ds, 3 p's sep. by 2 ds, 3 ds, p, 5 ds, cl. Rw, ch of 5 ds. R of 5 ds, join to p of adjacent r, 3 ds, 3 p's sep. by 2 ds, 3 ds, p, 5 ds, cl. Rw, r same as previous r. Rw, ch of 9 ds.

Rw, sr of 5 ds, join to nearest p of adjacent r, 3 ds, p, 5 ds, cl. Rw, r of 5 ds, join to p of adjacent r, 3 ds, 3 p's sep. by 2 ds, 3 ds, p, 5 ds, cl. R, close to last one, of 5 ds, join to p of adjacent r, 3 ds, 4 p's sep. by 2 ds, 3 ds, p, 5 ds, cl. R, close to last one, of 5 ds, join to p of adjacent r, 3 ds, 3 p's sep. by 2 ds, 3 ds, p, 5 ds, cl. Ch of 9 ds.

R of 5 ds, join to adjacent r, 3 ds, 3 p's sep. by 2 ds, 3 ds, p, 5 ds, cl. Rw, r of 5 ds, join to p of sr, 3 ds, join to nearest p of adjacent r, 2 ds, join to next p of same r, 2 ds, p, 3 ds, p, 5 ds, cl. Rw, ch of 5 ds. R of 5 ds, join to p of adjacent r, 3 ds, 3 p's sep. by 2 ds, 3 ds, p, 5 ds, cl. Rw, r same as previous r. Rw, ch of 5 ds. R same as previous r. Tie and cut. Continue thus, joining 2nd and 3rd p's of 1st r of each scallop to the corresponding 2 p's of last r of previous scallop.

No. 8831 . . . Use shuttle and ball of thread.

Sr of 8 ds, p, 8 ds, cl. Ch of 2 ds, 3 p's sep. by 3 ds, 2 ds. Rw, sr of 8 ds, join to p of 1st r, 8 ds, cl. Rw, lr of 5 ds, p, 5 ds, p, 5 ds, lp, 5 ds, sm p, 10 ds, cl. Ch of 3 ds, 3 p's sep. by 3 ds, 2 ds. Rw, sr of 8 ds, join to p of 1st r, 8 ds, cl. ** Ch of 3 ds, p, 3 ds. * Rw, lr of 10 ds, join to sm p of previous lr, 5 ds, join to lp, 5 ds, sm p, 10 ds, cl. Rw, ch of 3 ds, 4 p's sep. by 3 ds, 3 ds. Repeat from * once more. Rw, lr of 10 ds, join to sm p of previous lr, 5 ds, join to lp, 5 ds, sm p, 10 ds, cl. Rw, ch of 3 ds, p, 3 ds. Sr of 8 ds, p, 8 ds, cl. Rw, ch of 2 ds, 3 p's sep. by 3 ds, 3 ds. Rw, sr of 8 ds, join to p of last sr, 8 ds, cl. Rw, lr of 10 ds, join to sm p of last lr, 5 ds, join to lp, 5 ds, p, 5 ds, p, 5 ds, cl. Ch of 2 ds, 3 p's sep. by 3 ds, 2 ds. Rw, sr of 8 ds, join to same p where previous sr was joined, 8 ds, cl. Rw, lr of 5 ds, p, 5 ds, p, 5 ds, lp, 5 ds, sm p, 10 ds, cl. Ch of 3 ds, 3 p's sep. by 3 ds, 2 ds. Rw, sr of 8 ds, join to same p where previous sr was joined, 8 ds, cl. Repeat from ** for length desired.

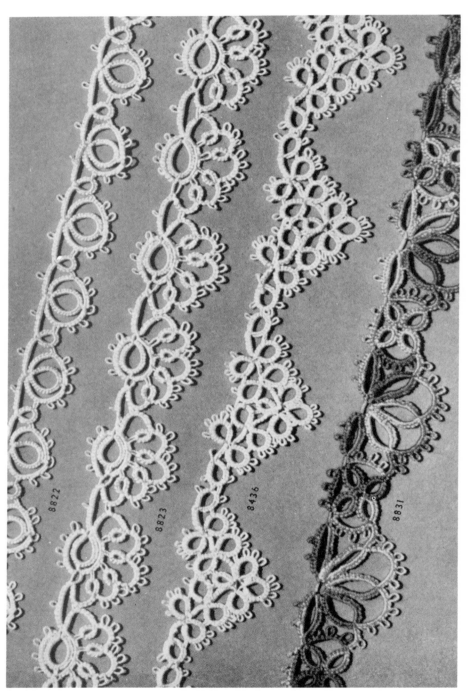

Filigree Edgings

USE J. & P. COATS TATTING COTTON

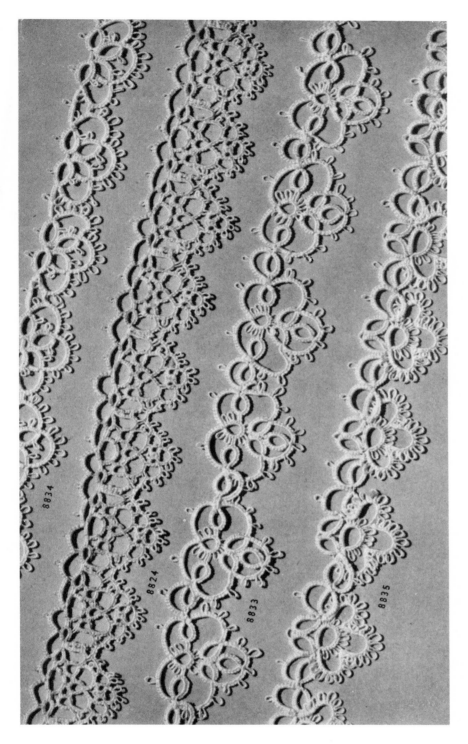

made on 1st row. * Ch of 2 ds, p, 2 ds, join to center p of next ch of 1st row, ch of 2 ds, p, 2 ds, p, 2 ds. Rw, r of 2 ds, join to next p of 1st row, 2 ds, p, 2 ds, p, 2 ds, cl. Rw, ch of 2 ds, 3 p's sep. by 2 ds, 2 ds. Rw, r of 2 ds, join to adjacent p of previous r, 2 ds, join to next p of same r, 2 ds, join to next p of 1st row, 2 ds, cl. Rw, ch of 2 ds, p, 2 ds, p, 2 ds, join to next p of 1st row, ch of 2 ds, p, 2 ds, skip 1 p, join to next p, ch of 2 ds, join to next free p. Repeat from * across. Tie and cut.

HEADING . . . Attach threads to 1st p of 1st r made on 1st row. * Ch of 5 ds, p, 5 ds. Rw, r of 6 ds, join to center p of same r, (4 ds, join to center p of next r) 4 times; 6 ds, cl. Rw, (ch of 5 ds, p, 5 ds, join to next p) twice. Repeat from * across. Tie and cut.

No. 8833 . . . Use shuttle and ball of thread.

* R of 10 ds, sm p, 10 ds, cl. Ch of 9 ds, p, 9 ds, join to sm p. Rw, r of 10 ds, p, 10 ds, cl. Rw, ch of 9 ds, p, 9 ds. Rw, make a center r of 2 ds, p, 2 ds, p, 2 ds, join to p of last r, 2 ds, 6 p's sep. by 2 ds, 2 ds, cl. Rw, ch of 9 ds, p, 9 ds. Rw, r of 10 ds, skip 2 p's of center r, join to next p, 10 ds, cl. Mark this r with colored thread. Rw, ch of 5 ds, 3 p's sep. by 5 ds, 5 ds. Rw, r of 10 ds, skip 1 p of center r, join to next (center) p, 3 ds, p, 7 ds, cl. Rw, ch of 4 ds, p, 4 ds, p, 4 ds. Rw, r of 10 ds, join to free p of preceding r, 10 ds, cl. Rw, ch of p, 4 ds, p, 4 ds, p, 4 ds. Rw, r of 7 ds, join to same p where last r was joined, 3 ds, join to center p of center r, 10 ds, cl. Rw, ch of 5 ds, 3 p's sep. by 5 ds, 5 ds, join to base of next r. Tie and cut. Fasten ball and shuttle threads to base of marked r. Repeat from * for length desired.

No. 8835 . . . Use shuttle and ball of thread.

* R of 12 ds, p, 12 ds, cl. R of 12 ds, sm p, 2 ds, 9 p's sep. by 2 ds, 2 ds, cl. Turn work and make ch of 2 ds, 9 p's sep. by 2 ds, 2 ds, skip last 2 p's of previous r, join by shuttle thread to next p. Ch of 2 ds, 9 p's sep. by 2 ds, 2 ds, skip 3 p's of same r, join to next p. Ch of 2 ds, 9 p's sep. by 2 ds, 2 ds, skip 2 p's, join to sm p. Rw, r of 12 ds, join to p of adjacent r, 12 ds, cl. Ch of 10 ds, p, 10 ds. Rw, r of 12 ds, join to same sm p where last 9-p ch was joined, 12 ds, cl. R of 12 ds, sm p, 12 ds, cl. Rw, ch of 10 ds, p, 10 ds, join to sm p of last r made. Repeat from * for length desired.

No. 8834 . . . Use shuttle and ball of thread.

R of 6 ds, p, 6 ds, p, 8 ds, p, 4 ds, cl. * Rw, ch of 3 ds, 5 p's sep. by 3 ds, 3 ds. Rw, r of 4 ds, p, 8 ds, join to center p of first r, 8 ds, p, 4 ds, cl. Repeat from * once more. Rw, ch of 3 ds, 5 p's sep. by 3 ds. Rw, r of 4 ds, p, 8 ds, join to center p of 1st r, 6 ds, p, 6 ds, cl (1st motif completed). Ch of 6 ds, p, 6 ds. R of 6 ds, p, 6 ds, p, 8 ds, p, 4 ds, cl. Rw, ch of 3 ds, p, 3 ds, join to corresponding p of adjacent ch, 3 ds, 3 p's sep. by 3 ds, 3 ds. Rw and complete 2nd motif same as first. Continue in this manner for length desired.

No. 8824 . . . Use shuttle and ball of thread.

1st row: R of 4 ds, 3 p's sep. by 3 ds, 4 ds, cl. * Rw, ch of 3 ds, 3 p's sep. by 3 ds, 3 ds. Rw, r of 4 ds, join to adjacent p of previous r, 3 ds, p, 3 ds, p, 4 ds, cl. Repeat from * 3 more times (5-r group made). R of 4 ds, 3 p's sep. by 3 ds, 4 ds, cl. Rw, ch of (3 ds, join to corresponding p of adjacent ch) twice; 3 ds, p, 3 ds. Rw, r of 4 ds, join to adjacent p of previous r, 3 ds, p, 3 ds, p, 4 ds, cl. Rw and complete a 2nd 5-r group as before. Continue in this manner for length desired. Tie and cut.

2nd row: Join threads to 3rd p of 1st ch

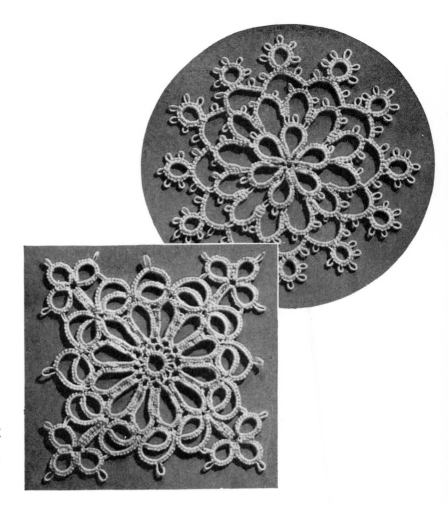

Snow Crystals

Delicate tracery patterns to hook together for doilies, luncheon mats, or to use as tiny coasters.

Round Motif

MATERIALS:

J. & P. COATS or CLARK'S O.N.T. BEST SIX CORD MERCERIZED CROCHET. If made in Size 30, motif will measure 3 inches in diameter.

Starting at center, r of 5 ds, sm p, 7 ds, p, 3 ds, p, 3 ds, p, 7 ds, sm p, 5 ds, cl. R of 5 ds, join to last sm p of preceding r, 7 ds, p, 3 ds, p, 3 ds, p, 7 ds, sm p, 5 ds, cl. Make 4 more r's like this one, joining the last r to 1st sm p of 1st r. Tie and cut.

1st row: Fasten ball and shuttle threads to 1st p of 1st r of center. Ch of 3 ds, sm p, 3 ds, 3 p's sep. by 3 ds, 3 ds, sm p, 3 ds and fasten to 3rd p of same r. Ch of 3 ds, join to last sm p of preceding ch, 3 ds, 3 p's sep. by 3 ds, 3 ds, sm p, 3 ds and fasten to 1st p of next r of center. Make 10 more ch's like one just made, joining last ch to 1st sm p of 1st ch. Tie and cut. **2nd row:** Fasten ball and shuttle threads to 2nd p of 1st ch in preceding row, ch of 3 ds, p, 3 ds, sm p, 1 ds. R of 1 ds, join to sm p of ch, 3 ds, 5 p's sep. by 3 ds, 3 ds, sm p, 1 ds, cl. Ch of 1 ds, join to sm p of r, 3 ds, p, 3 ds, fasten to 2nd p of next ch of previous row. Continue thus around. Tie and cut. If you wish to make several of these motifs, join them together at 2 r's on each side at center p's, leaving 1 r free between motifs.

Square Motif

MATERIALS:

J. & P. COATS or CLARK'S O.N.T. BEST SIX CORD MERCERIZED CROCHET. If made in Size 30, motif will measure 2½ inches square.

Starting at center, make r of 1 ds, 12 p's sep. by 2 ds, 1 ds, cl. Tie and cut. **1st row:** Fasten shuttle thread to 1st p of center r. R of 2 ds, sm p, 10 ds, sm p, 7 ds, sm p, 4 ds, sm p, 3 ds, sm p, 10 ds, sm p, 2 ds, cl. Join thread to same p from which r started. Carry thread to next p and fasten. * R of 2 ds, join to last sm p of preceding r, 10 ds, join to next sm p in preceding r, 7 ds, sm p, 4 ds, sm p, 3 ds, sm p, 10 ds, sm p, 2 ds, cl and join to same p from which r started. Carry thread to next p of center r, fasten and repeat from * 10 more times, joining the last r to the 1st and 2nd sm p's of the 1st r (12 r's in all). **2nd row:** Using ball and shuttle, fasten threads to 3rd sm p of any r of preceding row. R of 8 ds, join to 4th sm p of preceding r, 4 ds, join to 3rd p of that same r, 12 ds, cl. Rw, ch of 10 ds, p, 10 ds. Fasten to same 3rd p of same r. Rw, and make 2 more r's and ch's like those just finished. For corner, rw, ch of 5 ds, sm p, 4 ds. Rw, r of 8 ds, join to p of next to last ch, 4 ds, p, 8 ds, sm p, 4 ds, cl. R of 4 ds, join to sm p of preceding r, 8 ds, p, 8 ds, sm p, 4 ds, cl. R of 4 ds, join to sm p of preceding r, 8 ds, p, 4 ds, p, 8 ds, cl. Rw, ch of 4 ds, join to sm p of adjacent ch, 5 ds and fasten to p from which preceding ch started. This completes corner. Make another r like those already made. Ch of 10 ds, join to last p in last r of corner 3-r group, 10 ds, join to p as before. Continue working in this manner, making a corner after each group of 3 r's and ch's. Tie and cut. If you wish to make several of these motifs, join them together by the free p's all around motif.

Beautiful Tatted Edgings

Continued from page 72

FLEURETTE

No. 8437 . . . Worked with Tatting Cotton, this edging will measure about 1 inch wide. Use shuttle and ball of thread. **1st row:** * R of 12 ds, p, 12 ds, cl. Ch of 6 ds, 3 p's sep. by 6 ds, 3 ds, join to p of r, 3 ds, 3 p's sep. by 6 ds, 6 ds, join to base of r (a double ring made). Rw, ch of 6 ds, p, 6 ds, p, 6 ds. Rw, r of 6 ds, p, 6 ds, p, 6 ds, cl. Rw, ch of 6 ds, p, 6 ds, p, 6 ds, rw. Repeat from * for desired length. Tie ends and cut. **2nd row:** Tie threads to 3rd p of double ring at beginning of 1st row, make ch of 6 ds, rw. Lr of 6 ds, 4 p's sep. by 6 ds, 6 ds, cl. * Lr of 6 ds, join to last p of previous lr, 6 ds, 3 p's sep. by 6 ds, 6 ds, cl. Make another lr like this (a clover made).

Rw, ch of 6 ds, join to next free p of same double ring, 6 ds, join to first p of next r, 4 ds, join to next p of same r, 6 ds, join to 3rd p of next double ring of 1st row, ch of 6 ds. Rw, sr of 6 ds, skip 1 p of clover, join to next p, 6 ds, cl. Rw, ch of 4 ds. Rw, make a double ring. Rw, ch of 4 ds. Rw, sr of 6 ds, p, 6 ds, cl. Rw, ch of 6 ds, join to next free p of same double ring, ch of 6 ds, join to first p of next r, 4 ds, join to next p of same r, ch of 6 ds, join to 3rd p of next double ring of 1st row, ch of 6 ds. Rw, lr of 6 ds, p, 6 ds, join to p of sr, 6 ds, p, 6 ds, p, 6 ds, cl. Repeat from * across.

DEBUT

No. 8603 . . . Worked with Tatting Cotton, this edging will measure about ⅝ inch wide. Use shuttle and ball of thread. Sr of 3 ds, 3 p's sep. by 3 ds, 3 ds, cl. * Sr of 3 ds, join to last p of previous sr, 3 ds, p, 3 ds, p, 3 ds, cl. Repeat from * once more (a group of 3 sr's made). Rw, ch of 5 ds, 4 p's sep. by 5 ds, 10 ds. Rw, lr of 12 ds, join to free p of center sr, 6 ds, p, 6 ds, cl.

** Ch of 5 ds, p, 5 ds. Lr of 6 ds, p, 6 ds, p, 12 ds, cl. Rw, ch of 10 ds, join to next p of adjacent long ch, 5 ds, 3 p's sep. by 5 ds, 5 ds. Rw, group of 3 sr's, joining center of 2nd sr to 1st free p of last lr. Rw, ch of 5 ds, join to next p of adjacent ch, 5 ds, 3 p's sep. by 5 ds, 10 ds. Rw, lr of 12 ds, join to same p where center sr of group was joined, 6 ds, p, 6 ds, cl. Repeat from ** for length desired. Tie and cut.

FORSYTHIA

No. 8607 . . . Worked with size 30 Mercerized Crochet, this edging will measure about 1¼ inches wide. Use shuttle and ball of thread.

MOTIF . . . R of 8 ds, 3 p's sep. by 8 ds, 8 ds, cl. R of 8 ds, join to last p of previous r, 8 ds, p, 8 ds, p, 8 ds, cl. R of 8 ds, join to last p of previous r, 3 ds, 6 p's sep. by 2 ds, 3 ds, p, 8 ds, cl. Make 4th and 5th r's same as 2nd r. Tie and cut. Make these 5-ring motifs for length desired, joining 1st and 2nd r's to 4th and 5th r's of previous motif.

HEADING . . . R of 5 ds, p, 5 ds, join to center p of 1st r of end motif, 5 ds, p, 5 ds, cl. * Rw, ch of 8 ds. Rw, r of 5 ds, join to last p of previous r, 5 ds, join to next free p on motif, 5 ds, p, 5 ds, cl. Rw, ch of 8 ds. Rw, r of 5 ds, join to last p of previous r, 5 ds, join to next free p on same motif, 5 ds, p, 5 ds, cl. Rw, ch of 8 ds. Rw, r of 5 ds, join to last p of previous r, 5 ds, join to p which joins motifs, 5 ds, p, 5 ds, cl. Repeat from * across.

Tatting Instructions

TATTING ABBREVIATIONS

R . .	Ring	L P .	Long Picot
L R .	Large Ring	Ch .	Chain
S R .	Small Ring	Sp .	Space
D . .	Double or Doubles	Sep .	Separate
P . .	Picot	Cl .	Close
S P .	Short Picot		

TATTING

Tatting Shuttles are shaped like the *one illustrated*. Some are made with a hook at one end which is used to pull the thread through picots in joining. However, for a beginner the one without a hook is easier to manage as the hook hinders speed and is apt to be in the way. Instead of using the hook to pull the thread through in joining, a crochet hook or a pin may be used. For real dainty tatting use "STAR" Brand Tatting Cotton. It is made in white and a variety of beautiful colors. For heavier tatting use "STAR" Brand Mercerized Crochet Cotton sizes 20 to 50.

WINDING THE SHUTTLE

If the bobbin is removable and has a hole at one side, tie the thread and wind the bobbin until full. If bobbin is not removable wind thread around bobbin in center of shuttle but never allow thread to project beyond the shuttle.

The simplest form of tatting is the ring. This is made with one shuttle only. When making a design of chains and rings two shuttles or 1 ball and I shuttle are used.

When a design of rings worked with two colors is made. use 2 shuttles. While learning we suggest using "STAR" Brand Mercerized Crochet Cotton Size 20.

It must be remembered when learning to tat that the knot is made on the shuttle thread and not with it though all action is done with the shuttle thread. This is accomplished by easing the thread around fingers and pulling the shuttle thread taut.

DOUBLE STITCH

Unwind the shuttle so the thread is about 12 inches long. Hold the shuttle between the thumb and forefinger of right hand, with the thread coming from back of bobbin, take the end of thread between the thumb and forefinger of the left hand and pass it around the outstretched fingers, crossing it under the thumb. (Ill. No. 1.)

With the shuttle in your hand, pass the shuttle thread under and over the hand just below the point of fingers. Pass the shuttle between first and second fingers of the left hand, under shuttle and ring thread and bring it back over ring thread allowing the ring thread to fall slack by bringing the four fingers of the left hand together. (Ill. No. 2.) Pull shuttle thread taut and then spread the fingers of left hand till loop is close to fingers and thumb of left hand and pull tight. (Ill. No. 3.) The second half of the stitch is made in the opposite way. Allow the shuttle thread to fall slack, pass shuttle over ring thread and back under ring thread and over shuttle thread. (Ill. No. 4.) Pull shuttle thread taut and tighten ring thread until second half of stitch slips into place beside the first half. (Ill. No. 5.)

By pulling the shuttle thread, the stitch slips back and forth. If it does not, the stitch has been locked by a wrong motion and must be made over again. Practice the doubles until they can be done without looking at instructions. A picot is made by leaving a space between the stitches. (Ill. No. 6.)

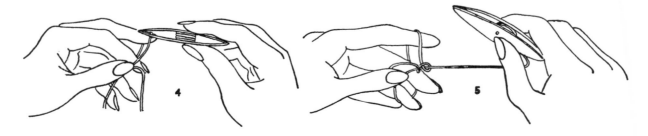

RINGS AND PICOTS

Make the first double as directed and work three **more** double stitches or doubles as they are usually termed.

PICOT. Make the first half of next double, slide it on thread stopping about ¼ inch from last stitch, complete the double and draw entire stitch in position next to doubles made. (Ill. No. 6 and 7.) Work doubles, then work another picot, work doubles, another picot and work doubles. Hold the stitches firmly in the left hand, draw the shuttle thread until the first and last stitches meet forming a ring. (Ill. No. 8.) For larger picots leave a larger space between doubles.

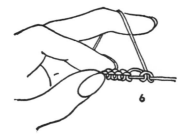

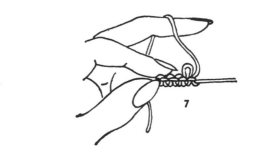

JOINING RINGS

Wind the thread around hand as for first ring and work first double stitch of next ring about ¼ of an inch from ring just made. Work three more doubles.

To join rings. If you are using a shuttle with one pointed end or a hook on one end, insert this end through the last picot of previous ring and pull thread through making a loop large enough to insert shuttle, draw shuttle through the loop and draw shuttle thread tight, this joins the rings and counts as the first half a double. (Ill. No. 9) complete the double, work 3 more doubles then a picot, 4 doubles, picot, 4 doubles, and close ring same as first ring. To reverse work, turn your work so that the base of ring just made is at the top and work next ring as usual.

To join threads. Always join thread at the base of last ring or chain by making a square knot and leaving the ends until work is finished as the strain of working may loosen the knot. Cut ends later. Never attach a new thread in ring as the knots will not pass through the double stitch.

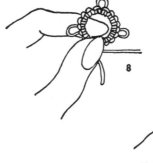

JOSEPHINE PICOTS

Single knots or Josephine picots. This is a series of single knots or just half of a double. Four or five knots for a small Josephine picot and 10 to 12 knots for a larger picot.

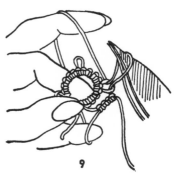

WORKING WITH A BALL AND SHUTTLE

All tatting designs containing chains and rings are made with one ball and a shuttle or two shuttles. To make a ring, the thread is wound to circle around the left hand and for the chain thread is wound half way around the hand. Tie the end of ball thread to end of shuttle thread. When you are making a ring use the shuttle thread, when ring is completed turn the ring so the base is held between the thumb and forefinger, place the ball thread over back of fingers winding it twice around little finger to control tension. (Ill. No. 10.) Work the chain over the ball thread using the shuttle thread. When chain is completed draw the stitches close together, drop the ball thread and with shuttle thread work another ring. Picots in chains are made and joined in same manner as in rings.

USING TWO COLORS

When two colors are used in making rings two shuttles must be used. If chains appear on the design with two colors use the second shuttle same as a ball.

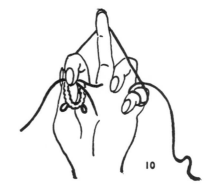

Metric Conversion Chart

CONVERTING INCHES TO CENTIMETERS AND YARDS TO METERS

mm — millimeters   cm — centimeters   m — meters

INCHES INTO MILLIMETERS AND CENTIMETERS
(Slightly rounded off for convenience)

inches	mm		cm	inches	cm	inches	cm	inches	cm
⅛	3mm			5	12.5	21	53.5	38	96.5
¼	6mm			5½	14	22	56	39	99
⅜	10mm	or	1cm	6	15	23	58.5	40	101.5
½	13mm	or	1.3cm	7	18	24	61	41	104
⅝	15mm	or	1.5cm	8	20.5	25	63.5	42	106.5
¾	20mm	or	2cm	9	23	26	66	43	109
⅞	22mm	or	2.2cm	10	25.5	27	68.5	44	112
1	25mm	or	2.5cm	11	28	28	71	45	114.5
1¼	32mm	or	3.2cm	12	30.5	29	73.5	46	117
1½	38mm	or	3.8cm	13	33	30	76	47	119.5
1¾	45mm	or	4.5cm	14	35.5	31	79	48	122
2	50mm	or	5cm	15	38	32	81.5	49	124.5
2½	65mm	or	6.5cm	16	40.5	33	84	50	127
3	75mm	or	7.5cm	17	43	34	86.5		
3½	90mm	or	9cm	18	46	35	89		
4	100mm	or	10cm	19	48.5	36	91.5		
4½	115mm	or	11.5cm	20	51	37	94		

YARDS TO METERS
(Slightly rounded off for convenience)

yards	meters	yards	meters	yards	meters	yards	meters	yards	meters
⅛	0.15	2⅛	1.95	4⅛	3.80	6⅛	5.60	8⅛	7.45
¼	0.25	2¼	2.10	4¼	3.90	6¼	5.75	8¼	7.55
⅜	0.35	2⅜	2.20	4⅜	4.00	6⅜	5.85	8⅜	7.70
½	0.50	2½	2.30	4½	4.15	6½	5.95	8½	7.80
⅝	0.60	2⅝	2.40	4⅝	4.25	6⅝	6.10	8⅝	7.90
¾	0.70	2¾	2.55	4¾	4.35	6¾	6.20	8¾	8.00
⅞	0.80	2⅞	2.65	4⅞	4.50	6⅞	6.30	8⅞	8.15
1	0.95	3	2.75	5	4.60	7	6.40	9	8.25
1⅛	1.05	3⅛	2.90	5⅛	4.70	7⅛	6.55	9⅛	8.35
1¼	1.15	3¼	3.00	5¼	4.80	7¼	6.65	9¼	8.50
1⅜	1.30	3⅜	3.10	5⅜	4.95	7⅜	6.75	9⅜	8.60
1½	1.40	3½	3.20	5½	5.05	7½	6.90	9½	8.70
1⅝	1.50	3⅝	3.35	5⅝	5.15	7⅝	7.00	9⅝	8.80
1¾	1.60	3¾	3.45	5¾	5.30	7¾	7.10	9¾	8.95
1⅞	1.75	3⅞	3.55	5⅞	5.40	7⅞	7.20	9⅞	9.05
2	1.85	4	3.70	6	5.50	8	7.35	10	9.15

AVAILABLE FABRIC WIDTHS

25″	65cm	50″	127cm
27″	70cm	54″/56″	140cm
35″/36″	90cm	58″/60″	150cm
39″	100cm	68″/70″	175cm
44″/45″	115cm	72″	180cm
48″	122cm		

AVAILABLE ZIPPER LENGTHS

4″	10cm	10″	25cm	22″	55cm
5″	12cm	12″	30cm	24″	60cm
6″	15cm	14″	35cm	26″	65cm
7″	18cm	16″	40cm	28″	70cm
8″	20cm	18″	45cm	30″	75cm
9″	22cm	20″	50cm		